And the Wind Blew Cold

And the Wind Blew Cold

THE STORY OF AN AMERICAN POW IN NORTH KOREA

by Richard M. Bassett with Lewis H. Carlson

The Kent State University Press   Kent and London

© 2002 by The Kent State University Press, Kent, Ohio, 44242
All rights reserved
Library of Congress Catalog Card Number 2002002001
ISBN 0-87338-750-3
Manufactured in the United States of America

06   05   04   03   02   5   4   3   2   1

Bassett, Richard M., 1928–
And the wind blew cold : the story of an American POW in North
Korea / by Richard M. Bassett, with Lewis H. Carlson.
    p.   cm.
ISBN 0-87338-750-3
1. Korean War, 1950–1953—Prisoners and prisons, American. 2.
Prisoners of war—United States. 3. Prisoners of war—Korea
(North). 4. Bassett, Richard M., 1928– I. Carlson, Lewis H. II. Title.

DS921 .B27 2002
951.904'27—dc21
2002002001

British Library Cataloging-in-Publication data are available.

To my wife, Valdeen, and all the wives of former POWs.

To our grandchildren: Hannah, Caleb, Alisa, Cody, Kara, Andrea, and Colton.

To the families of the 8,176 missing in action from the Korean War.

To my buddies from POW Camp Five, Pyoktong, North Korea, where the wind blew cold.

Contents

Foreword

by Lewis H. Carlson

I first met and interviewed Richard Bassett in 1998 while working on an oral history of Korean War POWs.[1] Richard had spent twenty-two months as a prisoner in what was to become known as "The Forgotten War." Like so many of the men I interviewed, Richard was reserved, somewhat reticent, and not a little distrustful of those claiming they wanted to hear his story. Former Korean War prisoners have reason to be suspicious. They remain the most maligned victims of all American wars. For almost half a century, the media, general public, and even scholars have, at best, described literally hundreds of these prisoners as "brainwashed" victims of a malevolent enemy or, even worse, as traitors who betrayed their country. In either case, these boys apparently lacked the "right stuff" Americans expected of their brave sons. That such accusations reflected exaggeration, distortion, and Cold War paranoia, rather than reality, mattered little to millions of Americans who saw their worst suspicions confirmed in the well-made 1962 film, *The Manchurian Candidate*, in which diabolical Chinese captors turned the minds of their American prisoners into Silly Putty before programming them to commit heinous acts against their own country. Many lesser films, countless novels and short stories, and sensational news reporting also contributed to this negative portrayal, as did the U.S. government itself. Then, too, there were the twenty-one Turncoats who refused repatriation in 1953, choosing instead to live in the People's

---

1. Lewis H. Carlson, *Remembered Prisoners of a Forgotten War: An Oral History of Korean War POWs* (New York: St. Martin's Press, 2002).

Republic of China. In truth, the other 4,418 surviving American POWS were thrilled to return home, but their stories have been largely ignored except for those very few later accused of collaboration.

No American prisoners in any war suffered worse conditions than those incarcerated in Korea. Many Americans are familiar with the harsh treatment the Japanese meted out to their captives in World War II, especially during the Bataan Death March, where fatality rates reached 40 percent. However, the 7,245 Americans captured in Korea suffered approximately the same overall death rate as did the Bataan prisoners, and the mortality rate among those captured during the first months in Korea exceeded 50 percent.

So it was no great surprise that Richard was hesitant to trust me. At the time of our interview, he mentioned that during a sixty-day convalescent leave in 1953, he had written a long memoir. His father and one of his brothers had looked at it, but no one else had, not even his wife, and he was not sure he wanted to show it to me. Nevertheless, several weeks later his personal story arrived in the mail.

What immediately impressed me about Richard's narrative was his scrupulous attention to detail and his ability to recall almost every day of his captivity. I asked him if he had a photographic memory. He laughed and said a college professor had once posed the same question. His story is of crucial importance because his comprehensive descriptions of Camp 5, which held more prisoners than any other Chinese or North Korean camp, cannot be found elsewhere.

Richard's narrative accurately describes the shock of the initial capture and the ensuing long march when so many prisoners died of unhealed combat wounds, disease, hunger, paralyzing cold, and brutal mistreatment. Even after arriving in a permanent camp, the trauma continued, especially when the Chinese attempted mentally to break down prisoners in the hopes of exploiting them for propaganda purposes. When conditions become so horrifying that survival itself becomes the sole operating instinct, men do break, as they have in all wars. Richard is candid about such behavior and condemns those who betrayed their fellow prisoners; however, he also understands that the behavior of most POWs reflects the conditions surrounding their captivity more than it does any personal shortcoming.

Besides such basic needs as food, clothing, and shelter, the greatest burden for most prisoners was simply boredom. Richard takes the reader through a typical day in a prisoner's life, including work, food, religious, social, and recreational diversions, and even those moments of terror when all hope seemed lost. Arguably, the most dramatic element of his story is the impact incarceration has had on his subsequent life. Richard wrote this part of his narrative almost a half century after his internment, and the reader will undoubtedly notice a very different tone from those sections written immediately after his repatriation.

After interviewing close to two hundred former World War II and Korean War POWs, I know the aftermath is the least understood consequence of having been a prisoner—and the most enduring. I also know that former prisoners are rarely ever again the same human beings. In this, Richard was typical. In 1978, he spent eighty-eight days in a Veterans Administration hospital for a wide variety of physical and mental ailments, including what would later be labeled Post-Traumatic Stress Disorder, all of which he candidly describes. To make matters worse, Richard, like so many of his fellow prisoners, was hounded for years by agents of his own government that wanted him to report on fellow POWs who might have done something wrong. Such harassment was a product of the McCarthy witch hunts and the paranoia of the Cold War, but its effect was to continue the victimization of the former prisoners. Richard also fought a long battle with the Veterans Administration to prove he deserved disability payments for his myriad physical and mental problems. What Richard and, indeed, all former POWs have been forced to endure should make the rest of us realize that these men have sacrificed far more than just the months, or even years, they spent in captivity. Richard himself put it best when he recently referred to America's national holiday commemorating its veterans: "Let me assure you as a veteran of the Korean War and as a former POW," he wrote in a letter to his local newspaper, "Memorial Day is not just a day off from school or work!"

Acknowledgments

I am indebted to Dr. Lewis H. Carlson for his encouragement, professional guidance, and editing skills. He suggested I add the Epilogue, he wrote the Foreword, and he contacted The Kent State University Press. Thank you very much.

To Dr. John T. Hubbell and the staff of The Kent State University Press, I am grateful. The helpful suggestions and, above all, their enthusiasm exceeded my expectations. Their suggestion to expand the Epilogue was a good one, and it will prove helpful to others who still struggle with the trauma of the POW experience.

Finally, thanks to my family and friends, fellow educators, and former students. Many of you encouraged me to "write a book!" What you didn't know was that it was already written, way back in 1953 while I was home on leave.

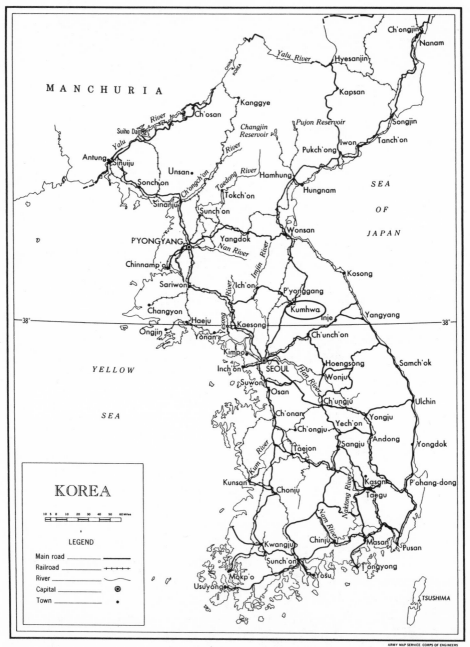

MANCHURIA

SEA

OF

JAPAN

YELLOW

SEA

KOREA

10 5 0   10   20   30   40   50   60 Miles

LEGEND

Main road _____
Railroad _____ +++++
River _____
Capital _____ ⊙
Town _____ •

TSUSHIMA

ARMY MAP SERVICE, CORPS OF ENGINEERS

The circled area indicates where I was captured on October 6, 1951. *U.S. Army Map Service, Corps of Engineers.*

Introduction

Why do the Heathen rage, and the people imagine a vain thing?
—*Psalms* 2:1

Why did Korea happen to me and thousands of other American boys? What were we doing some 9,000 miles from home in a prisoner-of-war camp in North Korea? These two questions occupied my mind for the seemingly endless days and fretful nights I spent in captivity. In my case the story started January 3, 1951, when I was drafted into the U.S. Army. I was one of the lucky ones because I missed that first terrible winter when so many of our men died on those blood-soaked hills and in North Korean POW camps.

We take for granted our many blessings and our high standard of living. But do we realize that, when the chips are down, we are soft? Do we really know what real poverty is? Do we understand that three-quarters of the world's population lives under horrible conditions that we Americans have never known? How many of us have any idea what it is like to be hungry and have no possible way to satisfy that hunger? Do we who bathe daily comprehend what it is like to be without soap? We sometimes complain of crowded living quarters without realizing that millions and millions of families get by in a single room much smaller than the average American kitchen. When at war, with our enemies existing under such conditions, how do we measure up when also confronted by such hardships? It has been almost 140 years since our own Civil War, when brother fought brother and their blood stained

1

America's hallowed ground. How would we react if, once again, we had to fight on our own soil, either against each other or some invading army? Pray God it never happens.

Basic Training

Cling to discipline. Do not relax your grip on it. Keep it because it is your life.
—*Proverbs 4:13*

Basic training! The date is January 3, 1951, and I have been selected by my friends and neighbors to be called to arms. It seems that in some little country in the Far East called Korea there is a civil war going on. I ask myself, what has this got to do with America? Since I cannot answer that question to my own satisfaction, I ask a buddy, but he doesn't know either. So I become real brave and ask my sergeant who has just returned to the States after recuperating from wounds received during the first month of the war. His reply startles me. In the unmistakable language of an old army man, he informs me, "You'll find out soon enough, and if you know what's good for you, you'll pay strict attention to everything in basic training because someday very soon what you learn here just might save your life." His words shock me, but I think, "Well, it will be all over in a few days, and at the very worst I'll just have to pull a little occupation duty until my twenty-one months are up; then, I can come home and forget all about it."

Basic training went on and on. I thought the army was trying to kill me before I even got to Korea. Those fourteen weeks seemed an eternity, and I wondered if I'd ever live through them. In truth, I was a softie. I didn't think so when I was back in high school playing football and basketball. No sir! I also thought I was pretty tough on those Boy Scout hikes and camping trips. But this was no longer play; this was training to kill. I didn't think much of the idea of ramming a bayonet through a canvas bag. That didn't appeal to me in the least, but the sergeant told me to think of that bag as an enemy who would kill me unless I got him first! That didn't sound like my high school coach telling me the importance of fair play and good sportsmanship.

When we started basic training, the boy in the next bunk was a great big, overweight guy, and I was as skinny as a rail. Funny thing, but by the end of those fourteen weeks we both weighed about the same. I also noticed that the climb up the hill to the barracks no longer left me panting for breath. Even the double-time and speed marches with full pack no longer seemed to bother me. Could it be that I was no longer soft? And all this time when I thought the sergeants were trying to kill me, they were actually doing me a good turn by not only building up my body but teaching me the value of teamwork and the importance of discipline. Of course, there were still thoughts of calling it quits and going home during that final week when we went on bivouac in freezing weather and on a midnight march because some guys in my squad refused to clean their equipment properly. Only later did I realize that this was all part of a program designed to harden us and to teach us the necessity of working as a unit.

After an extra week of pulling all kinds of dirty details, our orders were finally posted on the bulletin board. There was my name and beside it was something strange called FECOM. What in the devil was that supposed to be? Then I noticed that almost all my buddies had the same thing beside their names, which made me feel better. We soon learned that FECOM was just the army's way of saying Far East Command. Far East? Isn't that where Korea is? Oh well, the Far East is a pretty large area and includes lots of places besides Korea. Anyway, the Korean mess would soon be over, probably before the army could get us over there. Besides, we've only had fourteen weeks of training. Surely the army wouldn't send a bunch of greenhorns like us into combat! We'll probably get advanced training somewhere along the line, maybe Japan. Japan! The guys who have been there say they really like it so why start worrying about Korea? We're not there yet by a long shot.

Of course, the good news that I've been waiting for is that I will get to go home. So what if it is only for five days? I can see my friends and get some of Mom's good chow. I thought they were starving us to death during my first sixteen weeks in the army, and that the mess sergeant was paying for the food out of his own pocket. Of course, I had just gained more than thirty pounds, and there would be plenty of other things to beef about before I'd get out of this man's army; besides, when a soldier stops complaining, there's something wrong somewhere.

Five days never went by so fast. Then came the moment to say goodbye. I kind of expected Mom to shed a few tears, but what really threw me was the way Dad broke down. I told both of them to cheer up, that we'd probably only go as far as Alaska, and, anyway, in about six months I would be back home—a year at the most. Of course, I had no idea how long it would be before I saw those wonderful home folks again or what terrifying experiences I would have to endure before once again putting my feet under Mom's table. But, then, it was just as well that I didn't know what lay ahead.

I really enjoyed the trip across the States, except for those sickening moments when I thought about where I might be heading. Of course, I didn't know for sure, but there were those persistent signs that I might very well be going into combat, and that as an infantryman my chances for survival were not all that good. But it was spring, and that train seemed more like a string of Pullman cars filled with young men going to a college football game rather than off to war!

Traveling across America to our Seattle shipping port made me realize what a beautiful country this is, especially when cloaked in the wonderful garb of spring. The good Lord above had clearly blessed us with a country that most certainly was worth fighting for. But then something else began to worry me. I had been out of basic training for only two weeks, and already I was again becoming a softie. What kind of shape would I be in after the long trip across the Pacific?

Things happened fast in Seattle. We were processed and issued equipment, and, as always, there was that guy with a needle. We had already been shot so full of antibodies that I began to wonder if my body could possibly hold any more. We then moved down to the pier to wait and to grow softer yet. Finally, on May 2, 1951 we were assigned a ship and were ready to sail. The Red Cross arrived with its traditional coffee and doughnuts. There was also a military band that charmed us with its sentimental rendition of "So Long, It's Been Good to Know You."

We had just got nicely into Puget Sound, and I was in my sack thinking about home, when all of a sudden we rammed into the side of an oil tanker. For a few minutes there was great confusion. Almost immediately, an armed guard appeared in the stairwell and told everybody to get on life jackets and to sit tight. Excitement ran high when we were told that we would have to return to Seattle for repairs. But our delay only lasted twenty-four hours before we were put aboard a sister transport, although this time we left without the traditional coffee, doughnuts, and musical sendoff.

I soon discovered that life aboard ship was not very pleasant. I was assigned to the galley crew to help wash the thousands of dishes used for each of the two daily meals we ate. But what hit me was an ailment that made me wish, among many other things, that I was dead. I was seasick! Once out on the ocean, that little transport began to pitch, toss, and roll until I wished that I could be on any land—even Korea! Fortunately, about five days out of Seattle the sea suddenly lost its fury, and the topic of food no longer sounded so nauseating.

There were other things that got me hot and irritated, such as the fire drills when we had to don evil-smelling life preservers and rush up the stairwells to an assigned area on deck. We felt like we were old veterans, having already been involved in a crash at sea, so why bother with these annoying fire drills? The crowded quarters, rationed water, and daily inspections also served to keep us at odds with those in charge. Finally, after some sixteen long days, we landed in Japan. You would have thought that some of the guys had not seen a woman in the past ten years the way they carried on when they spotted some WACs on shore. Of course, the WACs were safely withdrawn before we hit land in military fashion—by the numbers.

Once on shore, we were surprised at the speed with which the army moved us about. We were put aboard a Japanese electric train and taken to an army post for the most rapid processing we had yet encountered.

Advanced infantry training at Station No. 2, Mt. Fuji, Japan, July 1951.

First of all, they hit us with a great big anti-malaria tablet, followed again by shots for any number of Oriental diseases—all this before we had a chance to get rid of that rolling, rocking ship movement and get our dry land movements re-coordinated. We also learned that just forty-eight hours after landing in Japan, we might well be going into combat! We turned in most of the equipment we had been assigned in Seattle in favor of battle gear. This, and a fast series of lectures on Korea and the army's procedures in Korea, ended any doubt about where we were headed.

It was also clear that our basic training fitness had worn off. We were ordered to fall out with full field equipment and sent double-timing to the rifle range to zero in our M-1 rifles. That was the toughest two miles of my short life, or so I thought at the time. I still remember what an officer said after half the guys fell out during our forced march to the rifle range: "You guys call yourselves men—and soldiers. Well, let me tell you, you're just a bunch of sissies. Furthermore, let me add that in less than six weeks half of you will be rotten dead." Then he added, "You think that little run was rough; just wait till you hit that rock. Now fall out again, and if any man drops out, I'll personally run him

First Squad, Mt. Fuji, Japan, July 1951. *Left to right: back row,* Singleton, Omar Serna, Roy Belcher, Umberto Capurro; *front row,* Fred Lavala, Arnold, Smith, Richard Bassett, Isaac Sandoval (not pictured). Squad members captured on October 6, 1951, were Serna, Belcher, and Capurro.

till his legs fall off." That night all of us felt homesick and not a little sorry for ourselves.

Early the next morning we were divided into two groups. The sergeant in charge of our group told us, "You see those men over there? Well, in less than twenty-four hours they will be in Korea. You guys are getting a break. You are going to receive twelve weeks of advanced training here in Japan."

At the time I really felt sorry for those guys and very happy that I was in the second group. However, in the next few weeks, I would many times wish that I had been in the first group. Our advanced training was many times more rigorous than was basic training at Fort Jackson. But then we began to hear about guys from that first bunch being wounded, killed, or missing in action. The war was getting close to home, and I hoped against hope that it would end before I had to land in Korea. But the weeks flew by, and it was painfully clear where we were heading.

At least we felt better prepared than those replacement troops who had been sent directly into combat, but no amount of training fully prepares a man for combat. One learns by personal experience and through the experiences of others. As a unit, we had only a handful of men who had combat experience and who knew the particulars of the situation in Korea. We had been taught to fight as a unit, to use the teamwork of the squad, the smallest of the infantry units, but I was soon to discover that when the big team lets you down, the squad sometimes goes to pieces, and then, like everything else in life, it becomes every man for himself.

Combat

The fear of the Lord is discipline, leading to wisdom, and humility comes before honor.
   —*Proverbs 15:33*

The trip over to Korea was even worse than the trip to Japan. Most of the other troops had traveled by train to the southern tip of Japan and then by ship across the narrows to Pusan. But we did it the hard way. We went back to the port of Yokohama and boarded another army transport. This was August 3, 1951, typhoon weather in the Orient, and we waited for two days for one to pass. Then we moved out and slowly followed this storm all the way around the tip of Korea and up into the China Sea. Finally, after four days at sea, we anchored in Inchon Harbor on the west side of Korea. Because of the terrific tides in Inchon Harbor, all the big ships had to anchor several miles out. We were herded into landing craft, and even though it was Korea, we were glad to get on firm land.

Inchon was not far from the infamous Thirty-Eighth Parallel. The smells in Japan had been different, but nothing like those in Korea. Immediately, I felt sorry for these dirty, hungry people who were dressed in rags and had no apparent roof over their heads. And the little children! How pitiful they looked and how many there were. After a brief march from the docks, we were put on a train, but it was a far cry from that Pullman we rode across the United States. We also got our first C-Rations. C-Rations are the old standby of the ground-pounder soldier: canned buffalo, fruit of the vine, dog biscuits in cans. Yes, good old C-Rations. Of course, in my haste to get at the contents, I cut my hand.

Our train was having a hard time building up enough steam to pull out, but finally, after a few bad starts and a long series of jerks, it began to roll, not at a steady or rapid rate, but it did roll. After some six hot, miserable hours and about one hundred stops for no apparent reason, the order came down to get our gear assembled, or, as the old cavalry used to say, "Saddle up!"

We were loaded onto trucks for what proved to be a dusty and nerve-racking one-hour ride. Our objective was a rock about eighteen hundred feet high located some ten or fifteen miles away. This was also to be our first real experience with the Korean terrain, which, simply put, consists always and forever of rocks, dust, or mud! And since the cooks had not had time to set up a field kitchen, the captain informed us that C-Rations would be the menu until the cooks learned how to keep up with the troops. After having devoted half the first night to guard duty and the other half to the mosquitoes, this announcement left us less than happy.

We did not immediately move up to the front lines; instead, we embarked on three weeks of maneuvers. We thought this was welcome news, but we didn't know how bad those three weeks were going to be or how hard our sergeants and officers were going to push us. The army seemed to operate on the theory that the madder it could make its foot soldiers and the less it fed them, the better they would fight. By the time we got up to the front lines, we were mad enough to fight not only the Communists but everyone and anyone who got in our way. It's a funny thing how this fighting business grows on you after training so hard and long and suffering all the abuse that ordinarily you would not take from anyone. After an infantryman has been kicked around a bit, he is ready to do some kicking himself.

I noticed right away that there were few, if any, Korean people in the area. Later we were told if we did meet any Koreans not to have anything to do with them. If we happened to bivouac in an area for more than a day, they would find us, and what they couldn't beg from us they would steal. So we were under orders not to deal with them and to run off any who might show up. This didn't seem right, but the army had very good reasons for such orders. Few of the civilians could be trusted, and since we were near the front lines, they had no business being there. After all, who could tell a South Korean from a North Korean?

We performed our maneuvers about twenty to twenty-five miles behind the front lines. Then I took what would be my last convoy ride in an American vehicle for a long time. Of course, at the time I had no idea this would be the case. The trucks drove us to within five miles of the front. We could now hear the big guns, and that night we didn't get much sleep. Before daybreak we were marched to the front. This time it was the real thing. They were now shooting back at us with live ammunition. While I was marching, I thought to myself, "Is it for this that my parents raised me and worked so hard to send me to school and taught me always to do the right thing? Was I meant to fight and die on foreign soil so that other men might be free?" Those and a lot of other thoughts raced through my mind after I began hearing the artillery shells.

The soldiers we were relieving were Turks. They were just having their breakfast, which consisted mostly of a loaf of fresh, hot bread. They offered me some, and, since they insisted, I took it. To my surprise, it tasted very good and I shared it with my buddies. Yes sir, those Turkish soldiers were glad to see us. They had been at the front for eighty-five days. Now they would go back to the reserve area and wash up and relax. Our platoon was assigned an outpost some 1,000 yards in front of the MLR (main line of resistance). Still further out between the MLR and the enemy was the Third Battalion outpost, which was manned by a whole company on a rotational system. Nevertheless, we didn't feel good about being out so far in front of our lines on our very first day.

We spent that first day getting our bearings, cleaning our weapons, working on our bunkers, and getting prepared for our all-night watch. Things were pretty quiet, or so I thought, for the outpost position. I could see a patrol coming in, and they looked tired. They had good reason to be because they had been out all night. They had set up an ambush just in case the Chinese decided to take over the battalion outpost during the night. This business of patrolling sent a cold chill down my spine. I wondered what it was like to be out there in no man's land looking for trouble. Well, there was no need to wonder for long. I soon had my chance to test the lessons that had been pounded into me back in Japan. A great rumbling in the distance and a cloud of dust told me that some of our tanks were moving into position for the night. Three of them came charging down on our position. I got the feeling they were headed for my bunker, but they turned off in another direction at the last minute.

As darkness began to fall on what would be one of the longest nights of my life, it began to rain. Already there was water in my bunker, and I had no alternative but to make the best of it. The mosquitoes were also out in force, and that dead cow about twenty yards away smelled terrible. When the artillery began sounding off, I couldn't tell who was firing at whom and whether it was incoming or outgoing "mail," as army slang labeled it. From somewhere over to my left came the chatter of small arms fire, but we were under strict orders not to get trigger-happy and start shooting at imaginary targets. Then my squad leader thought he saw something close to our bunker and told us to keep him covered while he investigated. Of course, all this made my knees play tunes while I broke out in the coldest kind of sweat. The squad leader's target later turned out to be an old truck engine, but just to be sure, he put a clip of forty-five slugs into it and came panting back to the bunker. Down about three bunkers I later heard two shots in the dark, and then someone started crying and yelling for the medic. On my very first night at the front, we had a casualty. One of the guys on watch had crawled out of his bunker to relieve himself, and on his way back his buddy, who had been catching a few winks of sleep, saw someone crawling into his bunker, got excited, and, without asking for the password or stopping to think, put two forty-five slugs into his friend who died almost immediately. This really upset all of us, and the poor guy who pulled the trigger went nuts. The platoon leader sent him back to the aid station, and the rest of us got our gear together. It was then dawn and all those nighttime targets turned out to be trees, bushes, and discarded equipment. Never have I been so glad to see the dawn, and never will I forget that first night on the front or be as completely shaken up. When our platoon was relieved later that morning, I was just as glad to see those boys as the Turks were to see us the day before.

After getting back to the MLR, there was hot chow that tasted wonderful, even though it was just powdered eggs. The best news of all was mail call, my first in Korea. There is nothing quite so dear to a soldier far away from home as a letter from those he loves. I thought the brass might let us rest after that harrowing first night, but I was sadly mistaken. There were more bunkers to be built or improved, weapons to clean, barbed wire entanglements to be placed, water and ammunition to be carried, and a thousand-and-one other jobs that always seem to face the foot soldier. So our routine was to work all day and stand guard all night. How they expected a man to keep going day and night for weeks at a time was a mystery to me, but somehow we did it.

After three days of this, we were told again to saddle up. It was our company's turn to take over the battalion outpost. This was to be the roughest part of the whole deal. We were to keep a patrol out front all day long. This meant that each of the three rifle platoons pulled one day of patrol while the other two platoons stayed in reserve on the outpost.

I will never forget my first patrol! Apparently, our side wanted to find out where the Chinese had their artillery, and our mission was to walk out there and give the Chinese a target so our own artillery could spot them and then knock them out of action. Naturally, our captain did not tell us this was our mission. In fact, he didn't tell us anything, nor did anyone else. Simply put, our job was to keep on the alert and to obey orders. That was enough for us to know. It was only later that we found out what our mission really was. So we shoved off the hill that served as our battalion outpost and began a cautious and slow advance into no man's land. For two or three hours we wound in and out of the rice paddies, expecting every moment to be our last, but all was quiet except for the heavy breathing of the patrol itself. To our left and right were mountains and several hundred feet ahead was a small hill around which ran a fast flowing stream. By this time we were five or six miles beyond our outpost. Then, at the edge of the stream, all hell broke loose. The Chinese had let us walk right into their lair, but it wasn't artillery they opened up with. No, it was mortars, and they were quite accurate. Lucky for us, it had rained the night before and it started raining again. So when those mortar rounds hit the rice paddy, they didn't do much damage. Nevertheless, when it also begins to rain mortar rounds, there are only two alternatives: advance forward or withdraw. Never, never dig in where you are or they will pound you to pieces. At the time we were in a prone position as close to that mud as we could get. To advance across the stream into the nest of Chinese would be suicide. To stay where we were along the end of the stream would be worse because we would all be killed before we could shoot any of the Chinese.

Our platoon leader passed the word for us to pull a strategic withdrawal, rather than a retreat. So with no further encouragement or prodding, we did an abrupt about face and advanced to the rear. The next thirty minutes were an eternity. It was a matter of hitting the mud, waiting for the round to burst, and getting up and running as fast as we could until we heard the next round coming in. Oh, you could hear them coming. They say it's always the one you don't hear that gets you. Well, those Chinese mortars followed us right across that series of rice paddies until finally we were out of range. The last man to join us was our platoon leader. Fortunately, there were no casualties.

That night the outpost was unusually quiet until almost dawn when somebody or something tripped over a booby trap about halfway on the other side of the hill. All the guys on that side opened fire for about thirty seconds, but that's all there was to it. Right after dawn, the captain sent a small patrol down to see what it was, but they didn't find anything. Often a rockslide would set off a trip flare or booby trap, and perhaps that's what happened. We had to be very careful when moving around because the front line area was heavily mined. We had to stick to certain paths. About 75 percent of the casualties among new troops were caused by mines or booby traps, so we learned to be very careful after a few of our friends got clobbered. And we would cover these so-called safe paths with a heavy crossfire if anyone undesirable moved along them.

At last our company was relieved from the battalion outpost, and we returned to the comparative safety of the MLR. By now there was some pretty heavy fighting around us, but fortunately not directly where we were.

Soon it was our turn to go out on patrol again. This time we advanced more cautiously and not nearly so far into enemy territory. This patrol proved uneventful; however, such days of quiet simply built up the suspense for the action we knew was coming. Another week passed, and I was counting the days until it would be our turn to be relieved from our front line duties and pulled back to a reserve area.

I was now a combat soldier, at least as far as the army was concerned, and I had to admit I was proud to be a member of a fighting unit. You never know what you will do under certain circumstances until forced to react, and I had passed my first test. About the middle of the third week we got a chance to go back to a little stream not far from the MLR where we could take a bath. This was a real treat, and we also got some clean fatigues. I felt like a new man. What I didn't know was this was going to be my last bath for a long time. I also received several nice letters, all of which greatly lifted my sagging morale. It was even pay-day. I sent my pay by money order back home. This was also to be my last payday until after my release on August 12, 1953.

On October 5 our company was sent back out to the outpost—for me it was to be the third and last time. It was a cold morning, and I had been in Korea for exactly six weeks, three of which had been on the front lines. Everyone seemed to have the feeling that we would run into trouble. The day before, the second platoon had run into an ambush and had to fight its way out. They did so but suffered one fatality and several injured. Their experience made us suspect that we might also be in for it. As luck would have it, the next morning we were the lead squad, and I was the fourth man from the front. It also happened that our platoon leader was not with us because he had been sent back to battalion headquarters to study the winter clothing situation. Our squad leader was also missing. Of all things, he had managed to go on sick call. So I felt rather alone out there, only I didn't know just how alone I would be before this day was done.

The weather was cold and foggy and we couldn't see much. The prospects of a successful patrol were slim, and everyone felt the tenseness of the situation. About a mile out, the platoon sergeant halted the patrol and called the squad leaders back for a conference. The rest of us were in a well-concealed ditch, so we took the opportunity to open a can of C-Rations and have a belated breakfast. The acting squad leader returned and told us we would wait for a while to see if the fog lifted.

That suited me just fine; in fact, I would have been willing to spend the whole day there. About nine o'clock, the order came down to proceed even though the fog was still quite heavy. However, there were signs of blue sky beginning to peek through here and there.

On these patrols we always maintained plenty of distance between each man so if the enemy dropped in some artillery or mortar rounds, not too many of us would be hit by the same shell. For some reason this morning the distance between us was greater than either necessary or wise. The two guys ahead of me kept looking back to see where the rest of us were. They tried to signal us to close our ranks, but if anything the distance grew even greater. After we had covered two or three miles, one of our light patrol planes flew over, circled, and suddenly sent a rocket into a hill about one hundred yards to our front. At the same time, small arms fire opened up on us. Everybody hit the dirt. In the confusion I couldn't tell what the situation was, but it seemed that the Chinese had set up an ambush and were firing on us from all sides. All of a sudden, I could see a bunch of enemy soldiers. I could even hear them jabbering away at each other. I tried to alert the acting squad leader, but after we fired several clips at them, the Chinese soldiers disappeared momentarily. They then returned fire from another direction that was far too close for comfort. While this was going on, I kept wondering what had happened to the rest of the patrol and why they weren't moving up to help us. Apparently, the six of us out on the point had been cut off from the rest of the platoon. This made me most uncomfortable, and those bullets kept coming closer. I spotted a couple more Chinese over to my right and fired at them. Then it became quiet and neither side was firing. I hoped that help was on the way and that maybe the Chinese had withdrawn. Unfortunately, that was not the case. When I tried to switch positions, the Chinese sent a burst of bullets right under my arm. My ammo was now getting low so I decided to withhold my fire. Then I heard one of the guys scream for help and call for a medic. I had last seen our medic at the rear of the platoon, and it was now clear that we were cut off and surrounded. All we could do was to try and get this wounded soldier to shut up before he gave our positions away. Things again became deadly quiet, and each minute seemed an eternity. Nevertheless, I was trying to analyze the situation while at the same time looking around without giving away our position. The path the patrol had been following was about two to three feet above the ground level of a surrounding rice paddy. It was only three or four feet wide with tall weeds on both sides. These weeds prevented the Chinese from seeing where we were lying. All this time I was praying hard that the good Lord above would get us out of this mess, but there just didn't seem any way out. To take off across the rice paddies would make us a perfect target, and to try to go back the way we had come would mean moving right back into their ambush. They had us right where they wanted us. If only the rest of the platoon could break through and get us out. Time, however, was running out, and we were increasingly helpless to do much about our situation. Not a sound was coming from the three guys in front of me, and I couldn't see the two guys behind me. It had been a couple of hours since we were first hit by the ambush, and my whole body was stiff and aching from lying so long in the same position. Especially my neck hurt from supporting that heavy steel helmet and liner. It felt like my head would fall off and roll down into that rice paddy. I continued to pray and think of home. I asked myself a thousand questions, but there were no answers. I had decided to get up and make a run for it when suddenly I saw two Chinese soldiers just on the other side of Omar Serna who was closest to me. One of them was a great big guy, and before I could warn Omar, they had captured him. Omar was now between them and me, and to fire at the Chinese would have meant shooting at Omar. I was about to roll off the path and down into the rice paddy, when they spotted me. There was no escape now. That big Chinese soldier raised his weapon, and up went my hands. Just as they were making both of us lie face down in the rice paddy, a single shot rang out, and without a murmur that big Chinese soldier fell dead at my feet, a neat round hole through his skull. But before I could get on my knees a half dozen Chinese were on me and immediately had the two of us double-timing across the rice paddy into the hills. The date was October 6, 1951, and I was a prisoner of war.

Captured and Marched

For the Lord heareth the poor, and despiseth not his prisoners.
—*Psalms 69:33*

It all happened so fast that it was difficult to realize just what a mess I had gotten into. A prisoner of war! Indeed, if anyone had ever told me that I would allow myself to be captured by the enemy I would have laughed right in his face. As a matter of fact, I had really never given the possibility a serious thought, and if I had, I would have said it would never happen to me.

Sometimes facts are hard to face, and this was one situation that I hoped was a bad dream. Yes sir, it is hard to face reality after all the props have been knocked out from under you. Here I was, in enemy hands, and no telling how long it would be before they did me in for good. What a heck of a way to go. Probably they would get all the information they could out of me, and then shoot me. The folks back home would never know what had happened to me. War is crazy business.

Our Chinese captors did not tie Omar and me up or even bother to search us. Once we were safely back in the hills, they put us in a cave and left us with this little guard with a burp gun as big as he was. After about an hour, someone came and motioned for us to come out and follow him. He gave us a slip of paper that stated in English and Chinese that we were now safely in the hands of the Chinese People's Volunteers and that we would be treated well and had nothing to fear. It also informed us that if we had any weapons, ammunition, knives, razor blades, or any sharp metals of any kind, we were to surrender them.

We were quickly searched and such objects were removed. They did not, however, take our dog tags. The Chinese were all smiles, and many of them wanted to shake hands. Clearly they were trying to impress us that they meant no harm now that we were in their hands.

Apparently the word had spread that two Americans had been captured, and more and more Chinese came in to get a good look at us. We felt like zoo animals on exhibit. We were then marched up this huge mountain. After about an hour of climbing, we were put in another shallow cave with another guard. We were thankful for the chance to rest and gather our scrambled thoughts. In less than an hour the first guard was back with a couple of tin bowls with rice and some kind of sauce. Fortunately, I didn't have to use the chopsticks he brought with it because I still had the little plastic spoon that came with our C-Rations. Either I was extremely hungry or the "chop chop" was good, or possibly both, because I polished it off in a hurry. Pretty soon the guard motioned for us to come out. He took us into a bunker where a very young-looking Chinese greeted us in perfect English. He immediately offered us a cigarette and extended his hand to shake ours and motioned toward a bench we were to sit on. Then he began to tell us almost word for word just what was on the piece of paper they had already given us. He acted somewhat timid and uncertain about what he was trying to say, and every few words he would stop and ask, "You understand?"

This little speech of his kept going around in circles, and if he told us once, he told us fifty times that we were not to be afraid but to obey orders and we would be all right. He said very soon we would be taken to the rear where we would be placed in a school so that we might learn the truth about the Korean War. He described this school as a large place where we would be issued warm clothing and given a comfortable place to live with plenty of good food. He told us we would be with plenty of other Americans and that as soon as we learned the truth, we would be set free and sent home where we belonged rather than over here fighting the Chinese who were our friends, not our enemies.

Well, all this bull and double-talk really sounded strange, and we wondered just who he was trying to kid. His little speech gave us plenty to think about, but, of course, we didn't believe a word of it. What we didn't know was that this was just the beginning of our interrogation and that this stuff was soon to become an old, old song.

Then came a surprise! Who should they bring into our cave but Umberto Capurro and Roy Belcher from our squad. We asked them about the other two guys. They told us both had been killed just after we were ambushed. We naturally hated to hear this, but maybe they were the lucky ones. They got it quick. They went on to tell us about how they had been captured. Belcher had plugged that big Chinese soldier who had captured Omar and me. They then slid down the side of the path and remained hidden for a long time. When they thought it was safe, they made a break for it across the rice paddies. They were making good progress when they were spotted by a Chinese patrol that opened fire on them. They were soon surrounded and Belcher was slightly wounded. By then everything had turned against them, and they were helpless to fight back. They surrendered. So there we were, four prisoners who had lost two of their buddies. We couldn't help but feel sorry for ourselves and think that the rest of the platoon had let us down.

About a half hour after dusk the Chinese decided to move us out. That first night wasn't so bad because we still had plenty of strength and were used to walking. They weren't taking any chances with us escaping so near the front lines. The guard in charge led the way, followed by two more guards; then came one American and one guard, one American and one guard, and so on. Bringing up the rear were two more guards. There was obviously no shortage of manpower in the Chinese army.

In Korea, the nights begin getting pretty cold in October. As long as we were marching, we didn't notice it so much, but when we stopped for a break, which we did every couple hours, the cold went right through us. This cold weather would soon be one of our greatest hardships. We only had our army fatigues and long johns, but very soon we would have less than that, and we were moving further and further north. Our prospects looked mighty bad that night, and the Chinese weren't fooling when they said to obey orders.

There would soon be many other hard lessons to learn. If I had thought for a moment that I would spend almost two years as a prisoner, I doubt I would have had the courage to keep on marching that first night. In the meantime, I had plenty else to think about. I thought about how I had been captured and what I could have done differently. I wondered about those other Americans "You Understand?" had mentioned and began to speculate on how long they had been prisoners. The war had been going on for almost fifteen months. Had some of those poor guys been prisoners that long? Funny that I had never seriously thought about being a prisoner before. I faintly remembered reading something about POWs while I was back in the States, or was it in Japan? Well, I would soon be meeting a lot of them and hearing their stories of starvation and near-death, but no amount of contemplating the other fellow's plight could take my thoughts away from my own troubles.

On and on we marched, and I began to wonder if the Chinese would ever stop again to let us take a break. When they finally did, I was so numb with cold that I wished we'd never stopped in the first place. We stumbled over rocks and slipped on ice until I didn't think I could take another step. Suddenly I heard the guide shouting something at what looked like another big mountain. After yelling like a crazy man for some ten minutes, he finally got a response from somewhere up on the mountain. We began to climb and climb. After a while we halted in front of a big ledge, and the guide went into a cave. He kept talking and talking and all this time I was getting colder and colder. I was just about to jump off that ledge, when he came back and motioned for us to move on. After some more climbing and twisting back and forth, we came out onto a sort of plateau where they put us in a shallow cave. This was to be our home for about a week.

It really wasn't much of a home, but that old cave was mighty welcome to a tired and cold group of prisoners. A blanket would have felt good, but either they didn't think of that, or didn't care, or perhaps they didn't have any to spare. We tried to get warm by huddling close together, which wasn't all that difficult because this was only a two-man cave. I finally managed to fall into a deep and troubled sleep just about the time the sun was starting to come up.

I was rudely awakened by a little, garlic-reeking guard who motioned for us to come outside. They had some chop chop for us. The other guards were already making a big noise over what looked like something the hogs back home would refuse to eat. And it tasted worse than it looked. This was our first meal of ground millet, steamed into a bread and stuffed with some kind of evil smelling greens. Immediately, we named them "mud balls," and mud balls they remain to this very day as far as I am concerned. Our C-Rations were a luxury compared to these mud balls; however, I soon had to learn to eat them, because I was going to see plenty more during the next thirty days.

In the meantime, the right honorable "You Understand?" had caught up with us and proceeded to tell us again about the wonderful Chinese People's Volunteer Army and its lenient treatment policy toward prisoners. He also wanted to talk personally with me. I couldn't disappoint him and suggest some other time because I was tired and had a headache. Actually, my first impressions of him were not that negative. He seemed quite friendly and sincere, but as the hours of interrogation wore on, my initial opinion of him changed considerably. His smiles and politeness disappeared, unless, of course, I agreed with everything he said or answered all his questions in great detail and to his satisfaction, which was almost impossible to do. The Chinese were great for details and repetition, and we were not prepared to deal with them. As much as I hate to admit it, they were very clever with their double-talk and very subtle in finding out just what they wanted to know. At first, I thought they were terribly stupid. Their initial techniques were so childish they seemed almost humorous. They would talk to us like we were children. However, "You Understand?" was not at all as simpleminded as he appeared. In fact, I completely underestimated his intelligence until I realized he had trapped me with my own words, and by that time it was too late to retract what I had said. I discovered the best policy in dealing with the Chinese was to appear totally uneducated and to claim complete ignorance. You then had to stick to this little game until you had them convinced that you were the world's thickest-headed creature. Then, and only then, would they leave you alone. (But I was wrong!)

Unfortunately, any mistakes during the first day of interrogation would follow me until the moment of my final release. The problem was that some of the statements "You Understand?" made called for a firm denial. I couldn't just sit still and listen to him condemn my government, our way of life, and our people without becoming angry and replying the best way I knew how. His response was not only to listen politely to everything I had to say, but to have me repeat it word for word so he could write it down. The problem was that my words then became part of the record the Chinese kept on all their prisoners and would later be used against me. Yes sir, these people knew what they were doing, and they were very thorough.

I knew that as a prisoner of war the only information I was required to give was name, rank, and serial number. It was certainly not my intention to give anything but that. For the first hour or so, "You Understand?" just talked about this and that, most of which simply repeated what he had told us that first evening of our capture, and I could get by with a few nods of my head and little else. But then he successfully dragged me into the conversation because I had allowed myself to become angry. Being an American, I was used to expressing myself quite freely. Soon all my intentions of playing it cool were shot, and I had allowed myself to become trapped in his little game of cat and mouse. Once I did so, there was no backtracking because the People's Volunteers, as they liked to call themselves, were like elephants that never forgot anything.

"You Understand?" seemed to have no conception of time, and his little cat and mouse game went on and on until I wondered if he were ever going to get tired and send me back to my cave. He finally stopped when an orderly informed him that mud balls were being served. This ended my first real session with him, but there was no doubt in my weary mind who had been the cat and who the mouse.

The other guys were naturally curious about my interrogation, and I was interested in their day. After choking down a small handful of mud balls with the aid of a cup of hot water, the four of us retired to our two-man cave. Our decision was not entirely voluntary. It was getting dark and cold, and our guard kept motioning toward the cave and raising his burp gun, so we got the idea. The other three guys had spent most of the day cutting dead brush on the side of the mountain, which became the fuel the Chinese chef used to prepare those exotic mud balls. When I tried to explain to my buddies how I had been trapped into talking too much, we were rudely interrupted by the guard shining a flashlight in our eyes and rattling off his mouth until I wanted to ram one of those big rocks down his throat. I understood enough to know that we were not supposed to talk but to go to sleep.

My second day as a prisoner was drawing to a close, and I got a funny homesick feeling in the pit of my stomach. This time of day was always the hardest for me during my many months in Korea. I would get the worst feeling that I was in the midst of a dark and troubled nightmare from which there was no escape. Sleep was difficult in any case in that cave. It was impossible to stretch out or to get comfortable. It was also cold, but at least it was better than the all-night march of the previous night. I even thought of the guard standing in the mouth of the cave. He had to watch over us while we were supposed to be sleeping. And what about the poor guy whose job it was to cook those horrible mud balls? It was bad enough to have to get them past your nose and down the hatch, let alone to have to stand out there in the cold over an open fire of brushwood and cook and smell those darn things all day long. Then there was "You Understand?" who had talked so hard all day long and was now probably spending his night bending over an old bean-oil lamp translating our conversation into some long report. And what of those Americans I still hadn't met who already had been prisoners for months? It was comforting to know there were some things to be thankful for even if I was crowded into a garlic-reeking cave, cold and hungry, and terribly homesick. Such were the troubling thoughts that raced through my mind before I finally dropped off into a fretful sleep.

It was still dark when the guard awakened me from a night of a thousand short naps. It seems every army has the same idea about when its men should rise and shine. To wake up to the sound of a bugle echoing its blasts off the side of mountains does have the debatable advantage that it really wakes you up. Once up, however, there was nothing to do except sit outside in the bleak, cold dawn and wish I were somewhere else. I never could understand why anyone should be rousted at 5:30 in the morning and be made to stand around in the cold with nothing whatsoever to do until 8:30 when our hot water and mud balls arrived. After our so-called breakfast, "You Understand?" arrived to talk to one of the other guys. I regretted that I had not warned my buddy about what to expect. On second thought, perhaps it was just as well because nothing I could have said would have changed anything. In such a case every man has to behave according to his own personality. I spent this third day of captivity with my other two buddies gathering brush and trying to keep warm.

The guard on our brush detail seemed a little friendlier than any of the others, and this helped. He seemed to be in no hurry for us to gather the brush so we just took our time and tried to communicate with him through a mixture of sign language, Japanese and Korean, and smiles. The guard broke down and even offered us a cigarette.

As the days went on I was to become more and more thankful that I did not smoke. It was extremely hard for those used to smoking a couple of packs a day—and even more under the stress of combat—to suddenly be without cigarettes. Being a prisoner simply compounded their misery. This desperate tobacco habit even caused some prisoners to start working for the Chinese. We learned that the average Chinese soldier got only one pack of cigarettes a week so for that guard to offer us a smoke was a considerable sacrifice on his part.

The day dragged on, and I was getting very hungry. Constant hunger pangs were something new for me, and I started thinking constantly of food and all the good things I would like to eat. The more I thought about food, the hungrier I got. I tried to put these thoughts out of my mind, but that was simply impossible. I even began to wish I had a mud ball to tide me over. Finally, the guard signaled for us to gather the brush and start back to our new home. On the way back we crossed a fast flowing stream, and despite the protests of the guard, we began drinking great quantities of that icy, cold water. Almost immediately I began to get the most severe stomach cramps I'd ever had. It seemed for every drop I had swallowed I now suffered about five minutes of severe stomach cramps. Clearly, cold water was not the answer to extreme hunger.

That evening we got something different than our usual mud balls. It was a grain about the size of a pea that turned a kind of purple when boiled. They called it barley but it was closer to sorghum. They served it with greens of some type, similar to those they used to stuff the mud balls. It didn't taste too bad, and it helped ease my cramps.

Once again, word had gotten around about us, and Chinese soldiers from the area made pilgrimages to see this curious bunch of "Mequas" as the Chinese called Americans. It was hard to say who looked the strangest, but since there was little else to do but stare and be stared at, we made the best of it.

My third day of POW life was drawing to a close, and as we four weary Americans got ready to crawl into our two-man cave, we wondered how long it would before the Chinese moved us to that camp where all the other POWs were supposed to be. Indeed, we wondered if there was such a place at all, or if they were just going to take us to a Siberia of their own somewhere deep in China. By now it seemed like I had always been a prisoner and that my other life was just a dream world that I had built up in my mind as a means of escape.

Before retiring that third night we ganged up on "You Understand?" and asked him for a blanket. For some mysterious reason this seemed to amuse him, although we saw no humor in our request. He assured us that everything possible was being done for our comfort and that he would personally check into this matter himself. Sometime during the night the guard shined his flashlight in our faces, muttered some words, and tossed something inside that resembled a blanket. It was not a real blanket but a poncho, which didn't do a whole lot of good for four men, but it was better than nothing. That night I was able to get a few hours of sleep so when the bugle blasted us out from under that poncho, I felt a little rested.

That morning, for the first time since I was captured the sun came out, and it was wonderful to catch its warm rays between the chilly blasts of wind. "You Understand?" was talking to his third victim, and the rest of us didn't have anything to do but sit on a rock and wish somehow we could trick old Mr. Sun into turning the clock back to summer. We spent three more days there, and each day seemed longer than the previous ones. By this time "You Understand?" had questioned the others and had each of us pretty well figured out as to our intelligence and general knowledge. On our sixth day the Chinese guards told us to take off our U.S. Army fatigues. In their place they gave us cotton-padded Chinese uniforms. You cannot imagine how thin a pair of pants can be and still hold together. They were reinforced around the knees and in the seat, and perhaps this is what held them together. The whole deal was humiliating. We were now wearing an enemy uniform, while losing our own, and our new uniform wasn't nearly as warm. But they were giving the orders so we had little choice.

That night we began marching again, and this time I discovered I was much weaker than during that first all-night march. A little moonlight helped as we stumbled wearily along the rocky mountain paths, but now my shoes were beginning to wear out. I had put in for a new pair of combat boots about a week before I was captured, but they had not arrived. I wondered who ended up with my boots. I had received my original boots during my first week in the army. Now there was an ever-widening crack across the back of both toes, which meant that every step I took pinched my feet. That night and during our subsequent marches I had serious doubts whether either the boots or I would hold out. We both did, but not without considerable pain. Of course, I wasn't the only one having foot trouble. The poor devils guarding us were marching along in thin canvas shoes.

We marched only at night because the Chinese had a lot of respect for the U.S. Air Force. During daylight they tried to keep out of sight. This was especially true near the front lines. When we got closer to the Yalu River and the Manchurian border, it became a little different.

Along toward morning we stopped at an old stable where we would stay for another week. Surprise! We were to share that stable with a mule and two other American prisoners. One of them was a master sergeant from Minnesota, and the other was a black corporal from St. Louis. We considered them be real old timers because they had been captured a month earlier. I'm not sure they were happy to see us because we woke them up to share the two blankets that they had previously had all to themselves. It is very hard to make friends and polite conversation at that time of night so everybody agreed to try and get some sleep. The hay we slept on was much nicer than the hard rocky floor of the cave, but, as with everything in life, there were also drawbacks. Since ignorance is bliss, we quickly and serenely dropped off into the warmest sleep since we were captured. At daybreak when our guards moved us—and even the mule—out among the rocks and trees until nightfall, we immediately discovered another surprise. Sleeping in the hay might have been soft and warm, but now we had body lice. These little creatures were to stay with us throughout that first winter, and they rapidly multiplied in the soft wool of our long johns. No longer could we complain about not having anything to do. As soon as the sun came out, we began our daily search for these critters, and on those days when the sun never shone, they would really get ahead of us. The days were getting almost as cold as the first few nights had been, and it was really a test of courage to remove your clothing to hunt for lice. But it had to be done. We could never really get ahead because each night sleeping in that hay furnished us a new supply of lice.

While we were staying at this stable, we were given our first lecture on the evils of capitalism and the glories of communism. This particular lecture was presented by a very high-ranking officer of the Chinese People's Volunteer Army. This joker had come a long way just to enlighten us, and we were told to give him all the respect due a high-ranking officer. He stood up and talked awhile in Chinese, complete with gestures and everything. Then another joker stood up and translated, complete with gestures. It was like a two-ring circus and was almost amusing except the Chinese are great for long detailed speeches, and this little lesson went on and on until I thought the two of them would never unwind. At last the session came to an end and everybody went away happy, we because it was finally over and the Chinese because they thought they had just won over some new recruits to the party line.

It was also at our stable stop that we came in contact with some South Korean prisoners. What we didn't know was that a couple of them spoke English pretty well and listened very carefully to everything we said and then reported it to the Chinese. We would never have known this except one of the other Koreans warned us to watch ourselves when these guys were around. Until then we had talked openly about our captors and, needless to say, it was not very complimentary. It came as

a startling revelation to realize that some of the guys who were supposed to be on our side were actually stool pigeons for the enemy. So
we learned to look around before we spoke and even then not to speak
very loudly.

While at the stable something else happened for the first time since I
had become a prisoner. I had my first bowel movement in almost two
weeks! This was not strange considering the complete change of diet
and the very small amount of food I had consumed. But once my bowels did start to function, they kept running night and day, and it was
only to get worse.

The word must have passed down from our former cave station to
the stable that we were not very fond of mud balls. For seven days,
morning and night, for fourteen straight meals, that was all we had to
eat. Although they contained little or no nourishment, it was necessary
to eat them even if you gagged on every mouthful. We were rapidly
losing weight and becoming weaker and weaker. Fortunately, we had
plenty of meat on our bones when we were captured or we would never
have made it. At least at the stable station we did not have to work, but
maybe it would have been better if we had. Lying around and thinking
how miserable you are is bad medicine for anyone.

We left the stable in a Russian truck for a most uncomfortable ride
that would last all night. The Chinese can put more men and equipment on any one truck than any other people in the world. Three more
Americans had joined us. They were pretty badly shot up and had been
in one of the Chinese front line aid stations since their capture over a
month before. That made nine Americans, six South Koreans, four Chinese guards, the driver, plus a truckload of equipment. We took off for
parts unknown, at least to everyone except the driver, and he wasn't
too sure because all during the night he would stop, get out and look
around, shake his head, and crawl back in. About four o'clock in the
morning the truck came to a final halt in front of several Korean shacks
alongside a stream.

We spent four or five days here. The Chinese were confused about
our arrival. Evidently they did not know we were coming and there
was no available room. For the remainder of that first night we were

put in the kitchen of one of the shacks. Fifteen of us were crammed into this one room, which could not have been more than ten by twelve feet in size. It was impossible to do anything but sit with our legs doubled up under us.

At this station I came in contact with the first Chinese woman I had ever talked to in my life. She was young and fat, and conducted my second long interrogation. She spoke very good English but very slowly. If I answered her by talking fast it made her very angry when she could not follow. Before long she was calling me a liar. To my surprise, this interrogation followed almost the same format that "You Understand?" had followed several weeks earlier. I noticed that she had some papers with my name on them in English with a lot of Chinese characters underneath. Evidently she was comparing my answers with the ones I had given to "You Understand?" No wonder she was calling me a liar, because all my answers could not have been exactly the same. Every so often she made a notation of her own on the papers, and I wished that I could read Chinese. For all I knew, she might have been recommending that they were wasting mud balls on me and that they should just go ahead and shoot me immediately.

That night we enjoyed a pleasant surprise when the Chinese gave us some rice and beans for supper. The chop chop here was the best we had had, and it was a lifesaver. However, before I could get started on my first bowl of rice, the South Koreans had already eaten up all there was left. This went on for about two days before we put a man in charge of rationing out the food equally.

I felt sorry for the GIs who had joined us just before we left the stable station. Their wounds had not healed. They were open and running pus and corruption. A Chinese medic stopped by to look at them, but he didn't have much to work with and probably wouldn't have known how to use it if he had. They never complained, but I could see they were in great pain, and I wanted to help them in the worst possible way, but there was not much I could do.

When I was captured, I had a New Testament in my fatigue pocket. It had been my daily habit to read it, and now I found myself reading more and more each day. I also was spending much of my time meditating on what I had just read. During my time as a prisoner, some of us would get together and study the scriptures, sing a few hymns, and pray. In those troubled times, it greatly helped to have faith in God and to believe that everything would be all right as long as we kept our faith. Maybe it had been the prayers of those who loved us back home that had preserved us in battle and were protecting us as prisoners. Prayer and religious fellowship brought me considerable comfort during my long months in captivity; in fact, I believe that the prayers of the folks back home and my faith in God played a tremendous role in my survival.

I was in my fourth week of captivity when, on a cold, misty afternoon, the Chinese moved us out on foot. This was to be our hardest walk yet. It was cold enough now that any moisture would freeze on the ground, and the mountain trail was slippery with mud and ice. But if it was hard for me, it was a lot worse for the wounded guys, one of whom had an injured leg. But our captors didn't seem to care, and once we started they expected everyone to keep up or else. When we reached our destination late that night, we found four more Americans prisoners so we were now thirteen. There were also about thirty more South Korean prisoners. We called this the rice station because every third or fourth day someone was sent to a supply point about seven miles away to pick up rice.

The Chinese moved all the Americans into one shack that had a million cracks in the walls through which the cold wind whistled; but for the rest of that night I was just happy to have a place to lay my head. These Korean shacks had a unique heating system, although possibly the oldest in the world. Under the floor of each house lay several clay or clay tile channels, the number of which depended on the width of the building. At one end of the building was a fireplace, which, in reality, was just a hole under the floor. At the other end of the building was a chimney. Theoretically, the heat and smoke traveled under the floor along these channels for the length of the building and then went out the chimney. In reality, unless the fireplace was enclosed, which often it was not, and the wind was in the right direction to drive the heat and smoke inward and the channels were tight and didn't leak smoke up through the dirt floor, you wouldn't get much heat. In the better Korean houses, the fireplace also served as the kitchen and was enclosed and the channels had a good strong draft. When that was the case, the system was effective, so effective that the floors would get so hot that if you lay on them you would get burned. Another problem was the fuel. It took an awful lot of brush to keep one of these fires going long enough so that the floor would stay warm for a good night's sleep but not hot enough to burn you. Because there was so little hardwood in Korea, we were not allowed to build a fire except during certain hours of the day. And if we didn't comply with this regulation, we got no fire at all.

It took a good part of each day to gather enough brush for our fireplace, a task made more difficult because we couldn't wander off in any direction we wanted. The Chinese set aside certain hours for brush detail, and we would all go out together and try to rustle up enough brush for a good warm floor that night. Not only was the brush difficult to obtain, but once lit, it was consumed in a flash, like putting wax paper into a fire. When we arrived that first night, we were soaking wet, cold, hungry, and completely exhausted. Fortunately, the floor was good and hot, which solved our most immediate problems.

On our first morning at the rice station the Chinese decided to stage a complete shakedown. This was something new, but in time we would get used to having all our personal belongings, of which we had practically none, displayed for our captors. They seemingly wanted a complete list of every item we possessed. Well, I thought, this won't take long, but it took much longer than I expected. For example, my wallet had to be turned inside out and every single item listed, even down to my pictures, money order receipts, and whatever else I had tucked away. I also had some things they just couldn't figure out, nor could I explain what they were. For instance, on my dog tag chain I had a small miniature of my automobile license. It was hopeless to try and explain this to the Chinese guard. He was convinced that a common soldier could not possibly own an automobile, and nothing I could say convinced him otherwise.

He also nearly went crazy when he had to list and describe my photographs. I discovered that most of these people were just thrilled to death with a snapshot. They would look and study them, smile and laugh, ask all kinds of questions, and then try to talk you out of them. One by one my photos disappeared. They also loved watches. When searching you, they would immediately lift up your sleeve and look for a wristwatch. Nearly all American prisoners had watches, at least when they were first captured, but only a small handful came home with one. On my final patrol my watch had gotten muddy and quit running. After seeing how excited my captors were about watches, and because mine no longer worked, I tossed it over the side of the mountain on that first all-night march.

On the third day at this station I went on my first rice run. It was quite an experience. The trip down was not so bad since it was daylight. It was raining and I did almost as much sliding as walking. The best thing was that the Chinese didn't make the wounded boys go, and it was a change of scenery for the rest of us. We had to stop several times and hide in the weeds alongside the path to keep from being spotted by Uncle Sam's jets. It is a very peculiar feeling to hide from your own planes. The Chinese had a unique warning system. On top of every mountain or hill they had guards who listened for planes. When they heard or saw one, they fired a single warning shot, which signaled all the troops in that area to take cover. The all-clear signal was two rifle shots. This system was surprisingly effective and saved many a life in North Korea, including my own on several occasions.

It was late in the afternoon when we reached our destination, which was a big supply point for the entire area. On the return trip, each of us had to carry one thirty-pound bag of rice. This time it was dark. At first that bag of rice didn't seem that heavy, but as time went on it got heavier and heavier. It was still raining and frequently I would fall, which meant my bag would take on a couple of extra pounds of mud. It was so dark, I couldn't see a foot in front of me. The path was also narrow and one wrong slip could lead to a long drop. I was extremely wet, tired, and happy when I finally got back late that night.

The next day we decided to try and patch up the cracks in the walls of our shack. If we had known that we would spend only one more night there, it is doubtful we would have started. It was another cold, miserable day, and by the time we had mixed up some clay and water and done a little patching, our hands were almost frozen, but nevertheless we managed to fill in the largest of the cracks.

The next day I received my first haircut as a prisoner. The barber was a Chinese guard who undoubtedly had no training whatsoever for cutting hair. (With the tools he had, training probably wouldn't have made much difference). He also volunteered to shave us, but only two or three of the guys were brave enough to undergo that ordeal. This barber also had the first piece of soap I had seen since I was captured. By this time I was getting pretty cruddy. Each morning I would go down to a nearby stream and wash my hands and face, but that didn't do much good without soap. I didn't even have a rag for drying off except for one very dirty handkerchief.

Once again we lined up for an all-night march, only this time we would march for three nights and each able-bodied man was given either a bag of rice or a bag of something else to carry on his back. Of course, we didn't know how long we would be marching when we left. The weather was now below freezing night and day, and those thin Chinese-issue pants were not much comfort. Another negative was that by now my bowels were so torn up that I had to go all the time. Because all the guys suffered pretty much the same way, our many stops made marching a terrible ordeal. Each night or early morning we would fall into an exhausted sleep in some Korean hut along the way. This was my first real contact with Korean civilians, and I couldn't help but feel sorry for them. The Chinese would arrive, and the Koreans would have to move their entire family out or into some tiny room. Sometimes there would be three or four generations in a single family. I could readily understand why the Koreans hated us, but they hated the Chinese even more. In many of the villages we passed through, the Koreans would spit on us and make threatening gestures. The Chinese actually had to protect us against the Koreans who would have gladly killed us on the spot if given the chance.

At the end of the third night we arrived in the largest town I had seen since landing in Inchon several months earlier. It was a mining town of some type and had been pretty well bombed out. While spending five days there, we were separated from the South Korean prisoners who had been with us since the stable station. Right after we arrived, each of us was given a set of Korean winter uniforms. They were khaki in color and consisted of padded cotton pants and a padded jacket. The padding was some two or three inches thick. These uniforms were very bulky and made moving awkward, but they did knock out a lot of the cold. They were not very clean and some had bloodstains on them; nevertheless, we were very happy to get them. This change of clothing also gave us a chance to boil the clothes we had been wearing.

We had to work in the mining station. The Chinese would march us out into the surrounding mountains, and we would have to drag back trees they had cut down. In our weakened condition, this was very difficult work. Just walking into the mountains would tire us out, but it was just another of those things we were forced to do.

The chow here was terrible. Every meal but one consisted of barley and some horrible smelling little crawfish that must have been ages old. The one exception was when we got our first bread made out of flour. Each man was given five of these most welcome "pancakes" and they were really a lifesaver. This station also boasted a Chinese doctor who came around every other day and dressed the wounds, which was a big help to the injured. During our third day there we were joined by a Puerto Rican prisoner, bringing our grand total to fourteen.

On the day we washed our old clothes we were told we would move out that night. There was nothing to do but pack up our wet clothing in a bundle. This time we would get to ride in a truck instead of walking. This was also to be the final leg of our journey north. It was to last for two nights and three days, and, like every leg, it too was to be an unforgettably bad experience.

The first half of the night we left was uneventful outside of the ride being extremely rough and crowded. Well after midnight we ran into a convoy of trucks moving south. The dust was so thick we could hardly breathe. The trucks were also moving with blackout lights, which was like having no lights at all. Suddenly, as we rounded a bend, flares lit up the entire area. Some of Uncle Sam's planes were following this other convoy and really giving it trouble. The bad part was that we had no place to go. I heard a plane coming right toward my truck with all guns blazing. One of the worst feelings in the world is being strafed by one of your own planes, but, of course, the pilot had no idea our truck was carrying Americans. The good Lord was still with us. Somehow those .50-caliber slugs plowed into the mountainside just to our left instead of into us.

It was about four o'clock in the morning when we pulled into Pyongyang, the capital of North Korea. At one time it had been quite a modern city, but now it was a bombed-out ruin. Our truck stopped on the edge of town, and we were put up for the daylight hours in a Korean home. We just got stretched out on the floor in time for an air raid. This was a bad place to be when Uncle Sam was dropping five hundred-pound bombs. One of these bombs fell not more than one hundred yards down the street, and it felt like it was a direct hit on our shack. After the building stopped shaking and things quieted down, I once again had to thank my Maker for sparing us.

While we getting ready to leave in the truck that evening, a jeep full of white men in strange uniforms came rolling by. It suddenly dawned on me that I had just seen my first Russians in North Korea. Not too far out of Pyongyang a truck full of Russian soldiers came alongside us, and they seemed almost as surprised to see us as we were to see them. Thankfully, the rest of that night passed without any further adventures.

We stopped about dawn in a little village of some fifteen or twenty Korean shacks. Again, the Koreans came from miles around to stare, laugh, and spit at the funny Americans. It was like being on tour with a circus. Instead of leaving that evening we stayed put until about four the next morning when once again we headed north. By now we were in very bad shape from all the travel and the month of near starvation. If we had been forced to walk that last stretch, many of us would not have made it.

We rode all day, and a couple of hours after dark we stopped for the remainder of the night. We were delighted the next morning when our interpreter told us that on this day we would arrive at the POW camp where all those good things were supposed to happen to us. I still had extreme doubts about anything good happening to me short of liberation, which didn't seem at all likely, but I was glad to get to any destination and just stay put for a while. It was a good thing, however, that

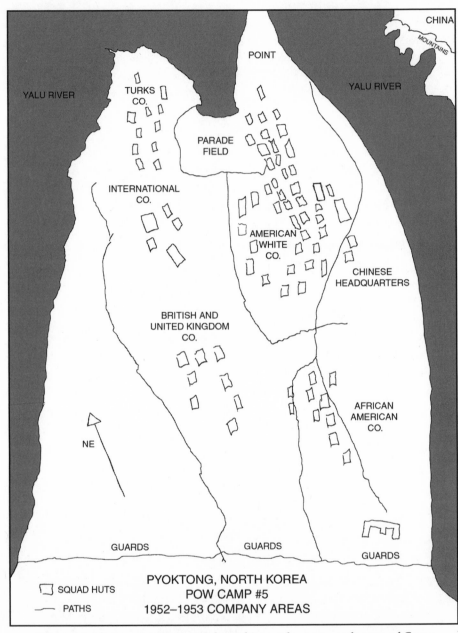

Fifty years after my internment, I drew this rough, not-to-scale map of Camp Five, Pyoktong, North Korea, as I remembered it in 1952–1953.

I didn't know I would be staying put for twenty-one months in this same camp.

About one or two o'clock in the afternoon we came to the end of the road. Ahead of us was one of the branches of the Yalu River. A barge landed and the truck drove aboard, and soon we were safely on the other side in a town called Pyoktong. Pyoktong, which was known as Camp Five to the non-Korean POWs and at the time contained almost two thousand prisoners, was on a peninsula across the river from the Manchurian border. It was about fifty miles east of the seaport town of Sinuiju, which was just across the river from Antung, China. The prison camp was located right on the point of the peninsula and covered about twenty acres. My first glimpse of the camp was from a hill over which the truck was slowly rumbling. We were just in time to see a large group of prisoners march out through the gates and down into the town. The date was November 6 or 7, 1951.

Overleaf: Camp Five, Pyoktong, North Korea. This photograph was probably taken by Frank Noel, a photographer who was captured by the Chinese.

Camp Five

Boast not thyself of tomorrow: for thou knowest not what a day may
bring forth.

—*Proverbs 27:1*

Pyoktong was as far away from the front lines where I was captured as
it could be and still be in North Korea (at least south to north). I figured
that from the time we were captured until our arrival at Camp Five, we
had covered some four or five hundred miles, much of it going back
and forth. The Chinese had apparently taken us northeast from the cen-
tral front almost up to Wonsan, North Korea, on the east coast; then
back down below Pyongyang; and finally north by northwest to
Pyoktong. Filled with the uncertainty of what was certainly a strange
new world, these had been the worst thirty days of my imprisonment,
but now they were behind me.

I will never forget my first impression upon entering Camp Five.
There was this haunted look on the faces of the men, most of whom had
been there for almost a year. They were little more than skeletons and
were suffering from malnutrition, starvation, and various other infir-
mities. My month as a prisoner had been nothing compared to the suffering, agony, and hell they had lived through. I felt like a raw recruit
among hundreds of twenty-year men. Most were not even of legal age,
but this living death had left its mark on them. They were now old men
in their late teens. It was many months before I completely pieced together their experiences and fully appreciated what they had gone
through. Some of them had been captured during the first months of

the war; however, the vast majority had been captured after November of 1950 when the Chinese poured across the Manchurian border into North Korea. Out of those captured during the first months of the war, less than half were still alive. Never have I ceased to be thankful that I had been spared the experience of going through that first terrible winter of 1950-1951.

Another group of prisoners had been captured in the big push of April 1951, and many hundreds of their numbers had also perished. The rest were like our group. They had been captured at various times and places along the front during the past few months. Those captured earlier were just as eager to hear our stories as we were to hear theirs, so we had plenty to talk about. The questions those guys could ask: they were not only starved for food, they were also starved for news of the outside world and, more particularly, of home. They were from practically every state in the Union and from many foreign countries. It was truly an international camp. There was so much to talk about that at times I almost forgot I was a prisoner of war in far away North Korea, hungry, cold, dirty, sick, and covered with lice.

I almost died during my first couple of months in Camp Five. I think I had yellow jaundice. Nobody in my squad thought I would live. I had also lost most of my hearing as a result of being bombed and strafed by our own planes on the long march to the camp. I spent that first Christmas of 1951 in what was loosely called the camp hospital. I remember Christmas Day: they brought me an egg, the only egg I had while a prisoner. I nursed that thing for two hours. Initially there were some American POW doctors at the hospital, but when the Chinese moved out all officers, we lost our doctors as well. Not many of our guys got out of the hospital alive during that first winter of 1950–1951. I survived (the winter of 1951–1952), but my hearing never returned to normal.

The Chinese put us enlisted men in a little shack right out on the point before we were moved into Company Three. The sergeants were taken over to the south side of the point and put into the NCO company. At the time, there were four different companies of men in Camp Five. First Company consisted of black, Indian, and Mexican Americans, as well as

French, Colombians, Puerto Ricans, Dutch, Australians, New Zealand-
ers, and many others; Second Company consisted of all Turks; our Third
Company contained white American privates and corporals, as well as
some two hundred English; and Fourth Company was made up of white
American sergeants. From time to time these companies would be moved
around and changed a bit, but this was the setup when I arrived. Each
company had its own area that its members were not allowed to leave,
plus its own kitchen, latrine, supplies, and Chinese officers.

When I arrived, our Third Company was the largest of the four with
over six hundred men. It would take a while before I got acquainted with
that many men, but eventually I was able to call practically every one in
my platoon by his first and last name and even nickname if he had one. I
also learned where they were from, their rank, their old outfit, how they
were captured, and hundreds of other little odds and ends. Some of them
would become my best friends, and some would get on my nerves and
rub me the wrong way; nevertheless, it was a good place to have as many
close friends as possible and to bear no ill will toward anyone.

During my first couple of days in Camp Five, the Chinese photo-
graphed me holding a card showing my name, rank, and serial number. This was followed by several short interrogations by a man who
would become my Chinese platoon officer. All my clothes were then
put into a big iron boiler and steamed out. On the third day I was assigned to a platoon and a squad.

Our company was divided into four platoons, each of which consisted of about ten squads, with approximately fifteen men in a squad.
I was assigned to the third platoon and the thirteenth squad (The Chinese numbered our squads; hence, we were Squad Thirteen, although I
was told that normally there should have been only ten squads in a
Chinese platoon). My squad had a three-room shack and sixteen men.
There were five men in each of the end rooms and six in the middle
room. I was assigned to the middle room, but I was not exactly a welcome addition because these rooms were very small. Our room was
about seven by ten feet. The two end rooms were even smaller. When
we all jammed in there, we could not move in any direction without
banging our heads or crowding our buddies. The building was very

low, and only in the middle could we stand up straight. It was just four walls, a roof, and a three and one-half foot door. This was to be my home for twenty-one months. Our shack was located high up on the northern slope of the peninsula. This was good because we had less of the dust or mud that was always around. On the other hand, being so high meant we caught more of the cold winter wind, but since it stayed below zero most of the time, a few degrees one way or the other did not make much difference.

Each platoon was responsible for all the areas surrounding its shacks, and each squad had its own smaller area. We had to keep our areas as clean as possible, and this occupied much of our time. Each morning we swept the squad area with a broom. If it had snowed during the night, we swept it up and carried it away, keeping the path as free as possible from ice.

When I arrived, the buildings and company areas were in bad shape, but the older prisoners told me it had been much worse when Camp Five opened. In the months that followed my arrival, we prisoners painfully rebuilt the entire camp. By the time we left in August of 1953, our camp was probably one of the cleanest villages in North Korea.

Our daily routine was one of never-ending monotony. Our day began at 5:30 when, instead of the usual bugle, a bell clanged. In reality, this bell consisted of a length of old window sash that the Chinese guard would hit with a good-sized rock. It was not exactly the most pleasant way to begin the day. However, it really woke us up. Immediately after the bell came roll call. Each platoon had an assembly area where we would line up in single file according to squads. Each squad leader would then report to the platoon sergeant the number present. When that was over, each platoon would march over to the company area where the complete company report was given to the company commander. This took five or ten minutes and was followed by fifteen to twenty minutes of exercises. We would then be dismissed or given a speech by the company commander or one of the company officers which might last anywhere from two minutes to two hours. All this time we were standing out in freezing weather wishing they would get finished so we could get back to our shack and out of that cold wind which always blew in from the mountains of Manchuria. What made these roll call speeches so unbearable was that they would first deliver them in Chinese and then in English. Besides being great for details and repetition, these people seemed just naturally to thrive on speech-making, and each of them thought he was just about the top speech-maker in the Chinese army. They could apparently do everything with words except stop uttering them.

Once roll call was over, there was very little to do except clean up our squad area, our room, and ourselves as best we could and then wait until 8:30 for chop chop. The food at this time consisted of barley in the morning with turnips and barley in the evening. About every fourth day we had potatoes or rice. The rest of the time we had steamed bread and turnips. These turnips were really something. (I'd have to be starving to eat another turnip!) During the late fall before the river froze, they brought in several large barges loaded with turnips. We would carry them up the hill to big storage bins, which, in reality, were large holes we had dug and laid logs across the openings. Naturally, when the ground froze solid, the turnips also froze, so all winter long we ate boiled frozen turnips. At least this was better than the mud balls and those horrible little crawfish we had eaten when we were first captured. The big treat was pork day. One hog for six hundred men does not go very far, so in order to stretch it everything about that hog except his last squeal was boiled for the troops. It was no surprise to find an eye-ball staring you in the face or see a pigtail floating serenely on top of the turnips. All food items were handled by the POWs.

The way the cooks killed and butchered the hogs before cold weather was quite a process. They would cut the hog's throat and dip him in a pot of boiling water. This would separate him from most of his coat of long, coarse, black hair. The carcass was then pulled out, scraped, and dipped again. They then removed his intestines, turned them inside out, and washed them. The rest of the process involved cutting the hog into small chunks about the size of a silver dollar, which were thrown into the pot to boil. After it got cold enough, the hogs that were to be used for winter would be killed and stacked up in a room where they would freeze. One would then be taken out, cut up, and cooked whenever pork day rolled around. As might be expected, it was a common thing to find a considerable amount of hair still on the pork skin when it came down in the soup buckets. Since meat was such a scarce item, we never let a little thing like hair come between us and our pork.

During the last week of November 1951, the Chinese issued us one pair of cotton-padded blue trousers and one jacket. This was the only clothing issued until May when summer blues were passed out. In order to receive the winter uniform, we had to turn in the Korean uniforms we had been given at the mining station. At least this was new material. We also received a cap with cotton-padded flaps, a pair of padded gloves, and a pair of shoes with rubber on the bottom and cotton-padded canvas on top. Because I got to Camp Five too late to be issued a blanket, I slept with my padded-cotton clothes on during my first winter. That same week we got our clothes. Each of us was issued a towel, a bar of soap, a toothbrush, and some tooth powder. I was very happy to see that bar of soap. It took me almost two weeks even to begin removing the layer of dirt off my hands because hot water was still not available.

Sometime after the first of the year someone located an old oil drum. The top was cut out and a fire pit was built around it. The primary use of the drum was to heat water for washing dishes, but on certain days we could get a pan full of hot water for washing ourselves. This was a real luxury. Each squad was issued a small aluminum pan that you could fight for with the other squad members when hot water was available. So, with patience and persistence the luxury of a "spit bath" could be yours providing, of course, you had not already used up your soap.

The method of preparing our food was very primitive. Each company had its own kitchen, which was simply a long shed with a series of fireplaces over which hung a huge black pot. Everything was boiled in these pots although occasionally our cooks, who were affectionately called "belly robbers," would get enough bean oil to fry the chow, which was something special. Each kitchen had its own crew and chief cook who were supervised by one Chinese officer and two Chinese soldiers.

There were water carriers who did nothing but carry water, wood chop-
pers who chopped the wood, and firemen who built the fires and kept
them going. All of these men were volunteers, and they enjoyed certain
privileges such as not attending roll call, pulling company details, or
having to attend certain lectures. As a group they were a good bunch of
guys who did everything they could to make our food go as far and as
equitably as possible.

Each squad had what was known as a room orderly. It was his job to
sweep up the squad area, pick up the chow, dish it out, clean up the
food containers, and wash the bowls. This job rotated day by day so
everyone had his turn. Each squad also had a chow box, which was just
a box with the squad number on it. Into this went rice, barley, bread, or
whatever we happened to have that day. Each squad also had a soup
bucket, again with the squad number on it. Into this went the turnips,
pork, potatoes, or whatever went into the soup. Each man had what
was known as a silver bowl, which in reality was a metal bowl about
two inches in diameter and two inches deep. Each of us also had a combat bowl that was a little tin bowl about one and one-half inches in
diameter and one inch deep. In addition to these two bowls, each man
had a tin cup and a spoon. This was our eating gear. When the chow
bell rang, all the bowls were set out in front of each squad, and the chop
chop was evenly distributed into the bowls. Each man got one combat
bowl of barley and one silver bowl of soup. If there was any left over,
seconds were distributed in the same manner.

The amount of chow that went into each container in the kitchen depended on how many men were in the squad. The chief cook had a
roster of each squad, and the chow was dished out accordingly. In our
squad everyone washed his own dishes, and the room orderly did not
have to dish out the chow if he didn't want to. If anyone did not like the
way the chow was distributed, he could take the bowl of the fellow who
was dishing it out. Each man had his own bowl, and each bowl was
marked so that it could be quickly recognized by its owner. Some amaz-
ing arguments came up over chow, especially on pork day. I can remember hearing about one involving this fellow from California. On one of

the rare pork days, it was his turn to go up the hill to fetch the daily food ration. When he brought it back, there was a hog's eye in his squad's portion. Well, when he ladled that eye into his own bowl, one of the guys took offense, and the two of them had a fight over that pig's eye.

There seemed to be no limit to the amount of barley some of those boys could put away. As soon as a squad's chow was gone, the heavy eaters would voice a very familiar cry, "Who's got any chow?" They would then make the rounds to the different squads just in case some of their buddies might have a little more than they could eat. The kitchen ran a roster on seconds, and if, after dishing out to all the squads, there happened to be anything left, it was given out as an extra scoop to whatever squads were due for seconds. If you were the one carrying food back from the kitchen to the squad, the guys would immediately ask, "Did you wait for seconds?" And if you happened to forget, your name was mud.

At first I wondered how those guys could eat this chow, but after a few months, I was able to eat almost as much as the best of them. For a long time, however, it was a matter of forcing myself to eat because each mouthful seemed to get bigger and bigger the longer and harder I tried to swallow it.

Barley coffee was our daily beverage. It was not much of a drink. The best thing you could say about it was it was hot and there was always enough left over for washing the dishes. The recipe was quite simple: burn some barley to a crisp, add water, then boil for several hours.

Our rooms served not only as bedroom, dining hall, and living room, but also as our washroom. It was a challenge to be able to take a "spit bath" without having the door opened at least twenty times during the process with freezing air blasting in with each opening. Despite the difficulties, it became a matter of pride to stay as clean as possible. Of course, there were those who just wouldn't go to all the trouble to stay clean, and since you had to live with them under very close conditions, it was not uncommon for the cleaner members of the squad to politely but firmly suggest that such members take a bath and clean themselves up. Staying as clean as possible helped get rid of the lice. The trouble was no matter how hard you personally might try to stay free of these little blood-thirsty creatures, if the guy who slept next to you had a colony of these pests, you would have them also. So it was a never-ending battle.

Back to the daily schedule: following breakfast was company detail time. This could involve the entire company or just a few men, depending on what work had to be done. About every third day there would be a brush detail. That's where the men were going I saw walking out of the camp that first day. Until the river froze over early in January, brush details involved a walk of perhaps five miles out into the hills and mountains west of Pyoktong. Each squad would usually send everybody but the room orderly to gather enough brush to last for four or five days. It would take about two hours to reach the area where we gathered the brush, another hour to gather as much as we could carry or drag back, and then two more hours to walk back to camp. In our condition this trip was no fun and often it was all we could do to get through it.

One of the room orderly's duties was to build a fire and keep it hot, but there were only three hours during the day when we were allowed a fire: two hours after morning roll call and another hour before evening chow. After the fire was put out, the orderly would rake the coals out of the fireplace and put them into a crude pan that we had made out of scrap tin. The pan of coals was then taken into the room, set on a couple of rocks, and everybody would gather around it and try and stay warm. Since there were three rooms and only two fireplaces in our shack, there was sometimes quite an argument over which room was going to get the hibachi.

During spring, summer, and autumn days when there were no brush details, there was usually some kind of work to be done around the company, such as digging a turnip hole, cleaning out the latrine, hauling rice or barley to the company supply house, unloading wood from the barges and carrying it up to the kitchen, repairing some parade field, rebuilding or repairing the ditches, walls, and walks around the company area, and numerous other tasks. At noon a new crew would come on to replace the morning one. Details were pulled according to a roster. Some days you might have to pull two or three details and other days none at all.

Every afternoon we waited impatiently for the 4:30 bell and the welcome call of "chow on the hill." The food may not have been much, but it was a long time between meals. Following the evening meal there was another roll call, and once again we lined up and were counted off. It was the same as the morning roll call except that almost always there would be a speech, usually about camp rules and regulations, which was repeated at least five times a week.

During winter evenings we could visit the various squads in our company until we heard the 9:00 bell. Then we had fifteen minutes to be in our room, ready to go to sleep when the final bell rang fifteen minutes later. Our platoon officer would then come around, shine a light in the room, and count noses.

Each squad was issued a small amount of bean oil for lights. To make a lamp we would take a combat bowl, fill it with bean oil, and make a wick out of an old shoestring or a wad of cotton. To light the lamp we took a piece of paper, ran with it to the nearest lamp, lit it, and ran back to our room before the paper burned our fingers. It generally took three or four trips before we finally got our light burning. To light the first lamp of the evening we would go to the kitchen where there was almost always a fire or perhaps we would find a few live coals in someone's hibachi. Sometimes we could even bum a match off a Chinese officer.

Almost every evening there was an air raid alert. The single rifle shot would sound off, and all lamps would immediately be blown out. As soon as the all-clear shots were fired, the whole process would begin all over again. You never got enough oil to keep your light going for very long, so you would either pool your oil for the evening with someone else or sit around in the dark and shoot the breeze about all the girls you had known or about something good to eat. Food and women were constant topics, summer, winter, spring, or fall.

Regardless of where one finds himself in this life, he will always look for an escape from reality. The escape in Camp Five was the terrible and poisoning habit of marijuana. This little, green plant grew wild in the hills of Korea and was found in abundance around Pyoktong. When we went out into the fields to gather brush, some of the guys were after something else to burn. It was hard to believe that such a habit could and did exist among friends and fellow Americans. Not everyone smoked the stuff, of course, but I was deeply shocked to discover how many did. Misery always seeks a companion, and the users of marijuana in our camp were no exception. In fact, on my very first evening in Camp Five some of the guys offered to treat me to a smoke. I couldn't have been more surprised had they produced a bottle of imported Scotch and offered me a drink. Thank the good Lord I had sense enough to refuse and to keep on refusing such an escape. It was a poor diversion, as one could easily observe from the effects it had on the guys who smoked it. This habit also helped explain some of the more haunted faces I had seen on that first day and in the days that followed. It would be difficult to say if it was the Chinese who got the men started on this poison, but it was plain to see that they did very little to stop or control it. Once in a great while they would tell the guys to leave it alone or even go so far as to have a shakedown and gather up all of it they could find; but, night after night, as you walked through the company area, you could very plainly smell the stuff.

Some of the guys would trade anything to get marijuana, even stuff that didn't belong to them, such as soap, tobacco, combs, mirrors, or anything else that was handy. If you hung any clothes out to dry, you either had to stay right there or get a buddy to stand guard so your clothes would not get up and walk off. Constant trading went on for other things as well. For example, during my first winter some guys traded military script, rings, watches, clothing, and even food for just a handful of tobacco.

The Chinese staged long series of compulsory lectures when all work would stop and everyone would have to attend with the exception of some of the kitchen crew. Our lectures were given by the chief company instructor whom we called "The Screaming Skull." His real name was Lin, Comrade Lin, as we had to call him. He probably weighed less than one hundred pounds. This little man with a giant voice was a very well educated Malayan and well versed in the theories of Marxism. His method of presentation was the most interesting thing about these cold and extremely boring orations. He had a masterful command of English and even GI slang. He also knew his history, except that his history had a most decided Communist slant. He could be very sarcastic and extremely degrading when he got wound up on the evils of capitalism, particularly the American version. On the other hand, he could paint quite an inviting picture of the glories of communism. It was funny how he could justify the Communists' complete domination of nearly half the world's people, yet accuse the capitalistic nations of trying to enslave the world. He undoubtedly believed what he tried to cram down our throats. It was always with great relief when we got out of these lectures and tried to forget this war of nerves. Day after day, he relentlessly pounded this communist theory down, around, and through our skulls. Repetition, repetition, repetition, until whether we wanted it to or not, unconsciously a little of this poison began to seep into our brain cells, although in our hearts we knew it wasn't true. This was just an attempt to get us to accept communist doctrines, and there was no escape from it. It was an almost-impossible job to sell us this stuff, because it was a rotten system that enslaved millions of people. The worst part of it all was holding our peace while our country, our leaders, our God, and our whole way of life were being ridiculed and condemned.

Sometimes the Chinese would get one of us up at one or two o'clock in the morning and grill us. They'd ask if we were Progressives. A Progressive to the Chinese was somebody who believed what they told us and would go along with them. They would try to get us to make broadcasts about what they called "The Chinese Lenient Treatment Policy," which, of course, was a bunch of bull. They also kept trying to get us to do things like draw maps of military installations. One night, just to get this interrogator off my back, I drew a map of Tampa Bay and told him it was an important military base. I had actually never been in Tampa. It was all a product of my imagination, but he thought my map was quite something. Of course, when he showed it to his superior officers, I'm certain they knew it was useless, but at least it satisfied this guy for one night.

Each of us was issued a notebook and a pencil. During lectures, we were told to keep notes. After the lecture we had to go back to our squad and discuss certain questions that the "Screaming Skull" gave us concerning that day's lecture. Each squad had a monitor who was supposed to write down the opinions of the men in his squad. These monitors would later be called to headquarters for a meeting. Needless to say, these discussion groups didn't amount to much unless, of course, our Chinese platoon instructor was sitting in on the session, which was often the case. They were always hanging around, telling us to go on with our "free discussion." It was "free" all right, as long as we said what they wanted us to say. Finally, after nearly a year and a half, the Chinese concluded that their little plan of study was not going over so well, so they changed their approach.

Some of the guys found a good use for the little notebooks the Chinese issued for taking notes during the lectures. They started using them for address books, diaries, and writing poetry. These poems were passed around and enjoyed by all. Most of them were about prison life and were not very complimentary to the Chinese. It was a dark and gloomy day when during one of their surprise shakedowns the Chinese gathered up these little books. Some of them were quite dear to the men, not only because of the time and effort they had put into them, but because they had artistically decorated many of them with beautiful, hand-drawn portraits and pictures

The next idea of the Chinese was to get the squad together and have compulsory group readings. Naturally, these readings were selected by headquarters and were very dull and strictly along party lines. This little plan also did not do well unless the platoon instructor was right there standing over us. Because there were so many squads in each platoon and only one platoon instructor, this plan had no chance of success.

Finally, the Chinese started a volunteer study group. Each of us was asked to join, but we could get out of it if we wanted to. Needless to say, only a few volunteered. They were mostly "Pro's" or "Progressives," as the Chinese called their favorite students, or a few curious guys who for various reasons sat in on some of the sessions. From this small group of Pro's came most of the men who stayed behind when it came time for repatriation. They were the big guns in the camp because they held all the good jobs, which often excused them from all details and roll calls. They were always having little parties of their own, complete with alcohol and plenty of cigarettes. They also had good chow and such hard-to-get items as matches, cigarettes, extra shoes and clothing, pen and ink, and an unlimited amount of writing paper. Many of their letters went directly home through China. They were also nearly always assured of plenty of letters at mail call. They were living proof of the lie that under communism everybody shares and shares alike. As long as they worked for and agreed with the Chinese, they received decent care. We also noticed the quick medical attention the Pro's received whenever they needed medicine of any kind.

The Chinese called the most strident anti-Pro's "Reactionaries." For them, medical care was just not available unless the Chinese feared one of them might die. Because there had been so many deaths by the time I arrived, the Chinese knew it was bad for their world image to lose any more prisoners. What's more, we were their bargaining pawns during the long, drawn out peace negotiations.

When we saw the favoritism the Pro's received, we became very angry, but there wasn't much we could do about it. One of the quickest ways to get thrown into solitary confinement was to offend or threaten a Pro. Fighting among the troops was strictly forbidden, but occasionally some of the guys would tangle. If the argument was between two Reactionaries, not much would be done except maybe a week of hard labor. But let a Reactionary touch a Progressive and that was another story.

The Chinese patiently continued to work on our indoctrination. The platoon instructors became very well acquainted with the men in their platoons and constantly worked on the individual in a manner calculated to win a new convert to communism. This was a painful process for both us and the Chinese. It was hard on us because we could not avoid these interrogations which sometimes lasted all day and well into the night. It was hard on the Chinese because at the same time they were supposed to be indoctrinating us, we were indoctrinating them. As a result, the platoon instructors were often changed because instead of winning converts to communism, they were becoming very confused Communists themselves. The only one who stayed consistent to the end was the "Screaming Skull." All the problem children were sent to him. He would plead, beg, threaten, and finally send a Reactionary back to his squad after lengthy sessions which could go on well into the night. Still, the Reactionaries resisted the Communist wooing. All this time the Pro's were becoming more and more deeply involved—some of them to the point where they couldn't back out even if they wanted to.

The Pro's were given a very chilly reception by the rest of the prisoners. It got to the point where no one would even speak to them, and so they became more and more dependent on each other and on the Chinese if only because they needed some companionship. When one of them would walk into an area where a group of men were talking, all talk would suddenly cease. When they would come back to their squads for meals or to go to bed, they would receive the cold shoulder.

It was very hard to comprehend why some of these men became stool pigeons. They would actually go to Chinese headquarters to inform on their fellow Americans. It was terrible that the rest of us had to be extremely careful what we said among our squad members or even in our room for fear of the guy next to us being a rat and reporting our conversation to the Chinese. Some of the snitches were pretty well known, but others were slick, undercover informants. It made me sick to think about it then, and it still does today. How could a man stoop so low for a few extra cigarettes or other special favors? We were really in the midst of a strange world where some of our fellow soldiers had lost all sense of duty and every vestige of rightness they may have ever known. What were the circumstances that brought about such conditions as these? Surely there had to be some reason for such behavior.

I heard this story from the lips of a hundred or more survivors of this nightmare. The roots of what happened could be found in that first terrible winter of starvation and death. This was not the whole story, however, because there were men who were captured later who turned bad and played into the hands of the enemy. I sincerely believe this rottenness had its roots in the desperation for survival. When men are facing almost certain death, is it not reasonable to assume that some of them would, in order to escape that death, be willing to sell their very souls? It was too bad that such things happened, but we must face the truth and learn how to prevent something like this from ever happening again. The conditions of the winter of 1950-1951 were certainly contributing factors for many of these men. Into the dirty, filthy town of Pyoktong, North Korea, came some 3,500 men. No one knows just how many there were because no accurate census was taken, even by their captors. It was early November 1950. These weary men had barely arrived in town when there was an air raid, and Pyoktong was bombed. Many of them were seriously wounded, but for them there was little or no aid. There was also little to eat, and what there was was not fit for human consumption. It consisted mainly of cracked corn and millet. The men would do anything to get something more to eat. One of them told me the story of a guy who even went around sifting through the vomit of POWs who had thrown up their food.

These men had also gone through some of the heaviest fighting of the Korean War. Many of their outfits had suffered close to 100 percent casualties. Day by day they were dying from their battle wounds, but their captors had shown little or no concern for their misery. The traveling and marching after capture had been extremely difficult. When they arrived at what was to become known as Camp Five, they were thrown into crowded, filthy shacks. Conditions steadily worsened, and more and more of them were dying. Some days as many as thirty or more were dragged across the ice and laid in very shallow graves on the side of the mountain above the banks of the Yalu. With guys all around dying, the others naturally wondered how much longer they could last. This went on until late in the spring of 1951. By then over half the original number of men who had marched into Pyoktong were dead, and their bones were being washed out to sea by the melting waters of the Yalu River. It was not a pretty picture. No words can describe such suffering. And this was just one prison camp. It happened in other places as well.

A man's life became of little or no importance to anyone besides himself. Under such circumstances how could any of them believe their captors when they started their classes on the merits of communism? How could they who had lived through so much go over to the side of the enemy that had allowed so many of them to die? In truth, many had started working for the enemy during that first deadly winter in order to gain what little favors they could. The seeds for their behavior were sown amidst the deaths of their fellow countrymen. The terrible part of this tragic situation was that once they started along this path, they could not back out, and so they became more and more involved in a very dangerous and treacherous game. But remember, it was only a handful who totally collaborated! The vast majority of our men showed an exemplary resistance and determination and never gave in to the torments to which they were subjected.

In the spring of 1951 this first group of prisoners noted a gradual change that coincided with the warmer weather. Those left alive went down to the Yalu River, cleaned themselves up as best they could, and then cleaned their shacks and the surrounding areas. With improved conditions, fewer and fewer of the men were dying. The food improved, and they noticed their captors were taking more of an interest in their living conditions. Some of the scars of that terrible winter began to disappear, but others would live on in the minds and bodies of those men for the rest of their lives.

About the end of November 1951 something happened that caused a great deal of speculation among us prisoners and caused our morale to improve considerably. Each squad was called to headquarters, and each man told to fill in his name, rank, serial number, and outfit on a piece of paper, not once but four different times. We didn't know at the time, but this was in preparation for the exchange of the names of prisoners on both sides that took place just before Christmas of 1951.

The Chinese also made all of us write our autobiographies. Many of us did such a terrible job that we were forced to rewrite them. We purposely told false stories or wildly exaggerated our pre-war lifestyles because we thought our personal lives were of no business to the Chinese. When we told our stories the second time, we naturally contradicted ourselves in a hundred different ways. This resulted in the Chinese having almost twice as many autobiographies as they had prisoners. Some of us had to write our stories four or five times, which was quite a challenge.

During the latter part of January 1952 the Chinese presented us with our first large mail call, which was an extremely happy occasion. They started letting us write home three times a month, but it depended a lot on what you wrote whether or not your letter ever left camp. My first news from home was indirect. Another prisoner had received a letter that included a clipping from my hometown newspaper, which made it clear that my family knew I was a prisoner of war. It greatly lifted my spirits to know that at least my folks knew I was alive. At the end of February I received my first letter. My mom had written it on New Year's Eve. One of the happiest moments a POW can have is to hear the mail clerk call his name. It was even wonderful to have fellow prisoners receive mail, even when you did not, because we shared our news from home with each other.

Until this first big mail call in January, only a few guys had received letters from home. Within a few months, we started having regular mail call every ten or fifteen days, and most of the guys got letters. Of course, their families had been writing; it was just that so many of these letters never reached us. I eventually received about forty letters, over half of which arrived during my last three months of captivity, and nothing did more to raise my morale. However, I can safely say I did not receive one-tenth of the letters that were written to me.

Once the ice was frozen solid across the Yalu, the brush details were easier because it was only a few miles across the ice to where there was plenty of brush in the mountains. These brush outings were not so bad because I was feeling better, and they gave me a chance to get out and break the monotony. We were guarded on these trips, but that didn't take away from a sense of freedom as we scrambled up and down the mountains. Some of the guys even made makeshift sleds on which they dragged their brush back across the ice.

We also hauled wood. During the fall and early winter before the Yalu froze, barges would bring in load after load of wood. The wood was used in the kitchens and consisted of small sticks about three or four feet in length. Each squad was entitled to so many "catties," or Chinese pounds, of wood per week to help keep the shacks warm. We would unload the barges and carry the sticks and pile them up behind the kitchen and headquarters. We had to climb about one hundred feet from the river to the hill. This was a never-ending chore because these sticks were quickly consumed in the hot fire, so it took many a barge load to keep the camp supplied.

Just as each company had its own kitchen, each company had its own woodpile. Whenever there was wood to carry, each man was assigned so many trips. There were checkers spotted along the path, and as you passed with a load of wood, you would be given credit for one trip. The system worked something like this: Each squad had a GI squad leader and a monitor who were appointed by the Chinese. Each platoon sergeant had an assistant platoon sergeant, both GIS and also appointed by the Chinese. The Chinese also appointed an additional man known as the DP for each platoon. His job was to serve as detail pusher and checker when there was wood to carry. Each platoon had a Chinese platoon instructor who could speak English. He had an assistant who was also a Chinese officer but who did not speak English.

There were quite a number of jobs in the company in addition to those in the platoons. Each company had its cooks, woodchoppers, water carriers, hot water pot detail, reporters for the daily bulletin and wall boards, librarian, show and recreation committees, mail clerks, and others for minor jobs. All of these positions were filled by GIS. At the company level there was a supply officer, a recreation officer, the chief instructor and assistant company commander, and a company commander, all of whom were Chinese.

Spring in North Korea came late but as such was all the more welcome. In reality, there were only two seasons in Korea: winter and summer. Beginning in early September, the cold weather lasts almost eight months, ending in late May. Summer begins almost immediately, but summer also is the rainy season. It can rain for days. By the first of July it is really hot and everything grows like crazy from then through August.

With the arrival of the heavy rains, we had to rebuild all the ditches, drains, paths, and walls around the camp. During the warm weather we cleaned up the camp from its winter accumulation of filth and trash. We had only the most primitive of tools so almost all work was done by hand. The shacks were all given a fresh coat of mud inside and out. Windows were knocked in the walls, and the fireplace covered for the summer. We enlarged the parade field and cleaned up and moved the latrine out on the point of the peninsula. The kitchens needed rebuilding, and all the roofs got a fresh layer of straw. Local North Korean civilians were brought in to do the roofs.

Each season had its pests. In the winter it was lice; in summer came the bedbugs, rats, and flies. To keep the flies down, the Chinese offered a prize of one cigarette for each one hundred flies killed. Even the guards took part in the fly killing. It looked strange to see a guard walking his post with a burp gun and a fly swatter.

It was a great joy to turn in our filthy cotton-padded winter uniforms and draw summer blues. Wearing one suit of clothing for almost seven months, day and night, was not the most pleasant thing in the world. For summer, each prisoner received two pairs of extremely lightweight pants, two jackets, a cap, a pair of light canvas shoes, two pair of shorts, and two shirts. In addition, each squad was given another wash pan, one comb, and a mirror. An extra ration of soap was also passed around, so when the river warmed up we could go swimming and get rid of some of the filth that had filled our pores during the long, cold winter. Each room was also issued new floor mats, which was a real treat. Because we had dirt floors, we used closely woven bamboo mats for floor coverings. The standard house rule was before anyone entered the room, all shoes had to come off. After all, this mat was our bed, as well as our table for dining, writing, washing, reading, and a hundred other things.

A group of us got together my first winter and formed a church. We held services regularly during the weekdays and on Sunday. The Chinese did not approve, but since they claimed everyone had religious freedom under communism, there were no grounds for them to stop us. They kept a very careful watch on our church group and often interrupted the services to summon someone outside. They would pretend they did not know what was going on and then proceed to question some member of the group. The services could only be held on a squad level, except on special occasions like Christmas, Easter, or Thanksgiving, when company services were held. As there was no ordained minister or chaplain in Camp Five, different ones among us would take charge of the services and do the best we could. We used some of the more familiar church hymns. There was also scripture reading and study along with prayer. I was privileged to preach the Christmas service in 1952, which was very ecumenical. Our services never attracted large crowds, but almost everyone in the company attended from time to time, and certainly these services meant a lot to those of us who regularly participated. The services were non-denominational, and everyone, even the Chinese, was welcome, although the Chinese rarely attended, and then I'm sure only to spy on us.

All I had was my little pocket New Testament, regular military issue, and one day a Chinese officer took it away from me. I went up to headquarters and complained to the "Screaming Skull." I said to him, "You told us we had freedom of religion and this is a religious book so I would very much like to have it back." He replied, "Go back, go back, go back!" He ordered me to go back to my squad. But three days later another Chinese officer, who was our platoon leader, returned it to me. I remember walking back from that Christmas service in 1952 with the "Screaming Skull," just the two of us, and I said something to the effect, "We appreciate you allowing us to hold this service." He didn't want to talk about it. Oh, man, he got mad and told me, "No! no! no! Go on and don't even walk with me." He then told me, "You are too religious." Although he certainly didn't mean it as such, I considered this to be a great compliment; in fact, if there was any single highlight during my imprisonment, that was it.

We played such sports as volleyball, basketball, and softball. Equipment was always scarce, and often the guys would make it themselves. The English and Turks were very fond of soccer, and spent most of their free time kicking a ball around. The Turks were also great for their style of wrestling. They would wrestle each other for hours. Occasionally, an American would challenge one of the Turks, who always insisted on their own style of wrestling. The Americans and the English liked to box and staged matches from time to time.

The British were especially good at presenting plays and really put on some good shows. Some Americans got up a hillbilly band featuring homemade banjos, guitars, and even a bass fiddle. Once in a while, the Chinese would show us a movie. Usually these were Russian propaganda films that supposedly portrayed life on collective farms or in state-owned factories and mines. Several of the Chinese films portrayed their successful 1949 revolution.

The Chinese also built up quite a library of books and magazines. Although most of the periodicals were published in either Russian or Chinese, one could still look at the pictures. As time went on, more and more English-language magazines became available. There were novels about Russia, China, and even the United States, as well as the complete works of Marx, Engels, and other Communists. Some of the Russian novels about World War II were fairly interesting. The few American books they had were written by Communists such as Howard Fast and William Z. Foster. We also had John Steinbeck's *The Grapes of Wrath*. Since most of the non-fiction books and magazines were strictly political, few of the guys read them except for the Pro's. The novels, however, were in great demand. I read a lot of books, and sometimes I gave a book review for the other guys. Interestingly, this almost caused serious trouble for me back in the States when someone reported that I was probably a Progressive because I had given these book reports. (See Appendix, document 3.)

The Chinese spent much of their spare time playing card games. During the summer of 1952, they issued each squad a deck of cards, which proved to be a popular way for many of the guys to pass time. The two favorite games were pinochle and canasta, with the latter introduced to the camp by the most recently captured men.

One of the oddities of prison life was language. It would have been next to impossible for an outsider to follow what we were saying. One could hear a great international mixture of Korean, Chinese, Japanese, Spanish, Turkish, American "bebop," and lots of profanity. Since the guys kept trying to outdo each other with pet expressions, this language kept changing in ways that only we prisoners could understand.

Prisoners spend a lot of time talking to each other about all kinds of things. I used to talk to this fellow we called Long Jack. He was about six foot, two inches, and I doubt he weighed one hundred pounds. He was the skinniest guy I ever saw. I'd tell him, "Long Jack, I think everything is going to be all right." (At the first reunion I went to back in the States I was walking into the hotel, and I heard somebody behind me say, "I think everything is going to be all right." I turned around and there was Ol' Jack. He remembered what I was always saying to him.) Jack was one of the guys the Chinese cut open under the ribs and inserted a chicken liver. This was supposed to suck out infection or anything else that was wrong. They only did this to the guys they thought were dying. It might have been an experiment. I don't know.

After the first days of March 1952, no new prisoners came to Camp Five. This meant there was little or no outside news except that which came in letters from home, but by the time they arrived, the news was already two or three months old. Then, too, the Chinese censors only allowed family or hometown news to get through. The only international news we heard was always about record crops in China, Russia, or in some Communist satellite country. Occasionally, the Chinese would pass out copies of the *Shanghai News*, which were usually a couple of months old. If you believed what was in the *Shanghai News*, there wasn't anything left of the American army in Korea. According to its statistics, the Chinese had killed more American troops than we ever had in Korea. They had also supposedly sunk all our ships and shot down every one of our planes. A typical story would describe some gallant hero of the Chinese People's Volunteers shooting down one of Uncle Sam's jets with his burp gun. Next to such an article would be a listing of the many thousands of casualties inflicted on the American forces during that particular week. Only three events of international importance reached the camp right after they occurred: the death of Stalin, the execution of the Rosenbergs, and the truce that halted the Korean War.

The only white woman we saw in North Korea was from the *London Daily Worker*. She was about forty-five years old but looked much older. When she walked through the British compound, the British prisoners yelled so many nasty things at her that the Chinese had to march her quickly through.

Because we had so little real news, the camp was one of the worst places for rumors. Some of the most fantastic stories made the rounds. One of the more unbelievable was that Luxembourg had declared war on England. Another choice bit was that General Motors was going to give all POWs a brand-new Chevrolet upon our return from Korea. Other rumors had famous movie stars killed in car and plane crashes, an imminent signing of the cease fire, huge plans for POWs after our release, and countless others too numerous and fantastic to be true, even to us.

About the middle of August 1952, the Chinese moved all the sergeants out of Camp Five and started a POW camp exclusively for them known as Camp Four. Camp Two was for officers, and Camps One and Three were for enlisted men. There were also smaller camps, as well as several large camps for South Korean POWs. After the sergeants moved to Camp Four, we were completely reorganized in Camp Five. The English were taken out of Third Company and formed into Fifth Company. First Company, which had consisted of international prisoners, became Fourth Company. The American blacks became First Company. The Turks were now in Second Company and the American whites in Third Company. Some of the English from Camp Three were brought up to Camp Five. There were several reasons for all this "Changey, Changey." From the Chinese viewpoint, the first and foremost reason was they hoped to improve the success of their indoctrination programs. They believed because the sergeants were mostly older men and held higher rank than the other prisoners, they were a bad influence on some of the younger men and kept them from accepting the Chinese indoctrination. And by breaking down the men according to their nationalities, the Chinese hoped they might achieve better results in getting the British to turn against Americans, the Turks against the other allies, the smaller nationalities to hate the larger capitalistic countries, and the black Americans to work against white Americans. Another less important reason was that the prisoners were too crowded and needed more room. The result was that each squad now had fewer members and more room. Our old Squad Thirteen became Squad Seven, and we now had twelve members instead of sixteen. This meant only four members in each room, which was a great improvement.

It was now well into September 1952, and the weather was getting cold again. We dreaded the thought of going through another winter, but there was no escape from our prison camp. Many men had tried to escape during the spring and summer, but none got very far, and all were brought back to camp and given sentences of between one and six months at hard labor. The major problem was we were hundreds of miles from the front lines (if you counted going up and down and around all those mountains). There was also the color of our skin, our bright blue uniforms, hostile Korean civilians, the food situation, the unforgiving terrain, the hostile weather, the insurmountable language barrier, and our weakened physical condition. Finally, there were thousands of Chinese soldiers between us and freedom. So escape was out of the question. Nevertheless, countless prisoners tried it, some as often as two or three times.

There was a punishment place known as the "hole" or the "icebox" where offenders of camp rules were put in solitary confinement. The icebox was a cement vault, and when it was ten below zero outside, it was twenty below inside this hole. In summer, those being punished were put in a shack with a solid door and no windows. In addition to this solitary confinement, there would be days without food or water, and what food one did get was not fit to eat. Some who were thrown into the hole were completely innocent of the charges against them. The Chinese were just trying to break what they called "their hostile attitude toward their benefactors."

By the fall of 1952, our general physical condition was better than when we first arrived, but it was still poor. Practically all of us had dysentery. When I really had it bad, I would go fifteen, twenty times a day. It felt like my bowels were going to fall out. I'd squirt a few drops and an hour later I'd have to do it all over again. The second biggest complaint was weak kidneys. Sleeping on the floor was largely responsible for this condition. Almost everyone had night blindness, which, while not painful, made it difficult to move about after dark, especially when walking to the latrine. Night blindness was caused by our poor diet, the lack of essential vitamins and minerals, especially vitamin A. This malnutrition also led to the "cracking" of skin. Another common problem was cracking in our lips, in the corners of our mouths, in between our fingers and toes, and even in our tongues. This was very painful and, most of all, made eating a difficult challenge. Other complaints were severe stomach cramps, dizzy spells, a general lack of energy, and constant fatigue. There were also cases of deafness and plenty of severe ear infections and toothaches. Several of the men began having epileptic fits and heart attacks, and some came down with tuberculosis. There were also numerous mental problems, such as general stress, severe anxiety and panic attacks, and even psychoses. There was a sick call, but the lack of medical supplies was still critical, so there was little relief.

With winter staring us in the face, it was again time to dig out the fireplaces, start going on brush patrols, and re-digging and covering the vegetable pits. There was also a new job. We had to dig air raid trenches all over camp. This was a complete waste of time and energy, but the Chinese insisted that it had to be done. About this time, the Chinese also tried to convince the world that the United States was using germ warfare in Korea. At first, we got many a laugh out of this. Every time someone found a bug or a fly, the rest of us would invariably make some comment about our air force comrades. As they had done so many times, the Chinese tried to convince us that when they repeated something over and over, it had to be true. By this time our lectures had begun tapering off, but when the germ warfare bug hit our camp, the old lectures started rolling again.

The Chinese took this opportunity to give us a series of shots. What these shots were is hard to say, but they were compulsory so everybody took them. They also gave us a blanket and a cotton comforter. This was of great help because now we could undress and still stay warm without having to keep on our winter clothes. The lice situation also greatly improved, and this also was a big relief. We had some hot water and a regular soap ration, so we could keep ourselves somewhat cleaner. Other items we received included tobacco and paper for rolling cigarettes.

We also got frozen potatoes instead of turnips for the winter of 1952–1953. This was a wonderful improvement, and there were others. The cooks had built an oven so now they could bake bread instead of steaming it. The flour ration per man greatly increased, and bread became a daily item; in fact, we had bread or rice for every meal. We also got more pork per man, and the Chinese increased our bean oil allowance. Finally, barley was now used only for making coffee. So in the mornings we usually had rice and soybeans. In the evening it was potatoes, bread, and sometimes pork. These potatoes were very small, and many of them had started to rot before they froze, but they were still better than eating frozen turnips.

Generally speaking, the conditions were much improved and made getting through the cold winter easier and more tolerable. We even got electric lights in one of the warehouses, which was then turned into a sort of recreation hall where we could spend the long winter evenings playing checkers, chess, and cards. We also made a ping-pong table, and the Chinese introduced us to Chinese pool, which is played on a small flat board with four pockets. Things had drastically changed since that first horrible winter of 1950–1951 and even since my first winter a year later.

About this time, the U.S. Air Force really stepped up what the Chinese called "the wanton bombing of innocent women and children." But what Uncle Sam was really after was the movement of Chinese troops. Hardly a day went by without us having a ringside seat to some spectacular dogfights between U.S. jets and the Russian-built MIG fighters. It was almost impossible to tell who was who, but we could see the tracer bullets flying and hear the nose cannons sounding off. Every once in a while we would see a plane go down in a blaze of smoke, and once not far from our camp a downed flyer drifted to earth in his parachute. There was also a plane that crashed into the side of the mountain just across the Yalu River northwest of Camp Five, close enough for us to hear. Most of the air raids took place at night, and we could see the bomb flashes, the searchlights, and the anti-aircraft bursts. It was quite a show.

It became difficult to remember that you had once been a free man, living in a free world with plenty to eat and plenty to do, a world in which you could come and go as you pleased, say what you wished, walk into a room, pick up a good magazine, flip a switch, flood the room with light, turn on the radio and get some nice soft music, lean back in that easy chair, and really relax without a thought that somewhere in the world men were fighting, becoming prisoners of war, and dying. All those precious things we had been brought up to take for granted were a way of life that involved only a very small corner of the globe. Imagine crawling into a bed at night between two nice, clean sheets, getting up in the morning to the tune of some soft dreamy song, taking a refreshing hot shower, having anything you wanted for breakfast, hopping into a nice new car, and driving off to work in a modern factory or office. We would drop off at night into a sleep with thoughts like these only to be interrupted by a half dozen or more trips to the latrine, and then wake in the morning to the reality of a clanging bell and some Chinese officer hurrying us to roll call, exercises, and propaganda in the cold darkness of a bitter winter morning.

Somehow the days faded into weeks and the weeks into months until finally the ice and snow began to melt and a bit of green grass appeared in our bleak and frozen world. The spring and summer of 1953 were to be wonderful for me and thousands of other men. Of course, we had no way of knowing what was going on in the outside world except for what our captors wanted us to know. If anything bad happened in the capitalistic world, we heard about it. If anything happened in the Communist world that they considered good, we also heard about it. Such was the situation that very late and reluctant spring of 1953. The cold weather just stayed on and on until finally in June the sun came out to warm our cold, homesick bodies; however, soon events would warm us in ways the sun never could.

Repatriation

Rejoice evermore
—*1 Thessalonians 5:16*

In early April 1953, we heard the news that was almost too good to be true. On a quiet Sunday, the loudspeaker announced there would be an exchange of sick and wounded prisoners. This was a complete surprise to us and started a lot of speculation. Who would get to go, how many would be included, and when would it happen? However, the way the exchange was handled made most of us lose heart and any hesitant respect we still might have had for the Chinese way of doing things. First they gave most of their favorite boys, the Pro's, a physical examination because the prisoners picked for this exchange came mostly from this group. This is not to say that all of those sent home in Operation Little Switch were Pro's, but many were. What really made the rest of us angry was that some of the sickest men in our camp were left behind so those Pro's could be repatriated. Still, it did our hearts good to see that some who had really suffered the most were going home, and everyone who knew any of these deserving men sent messages with them for their loved ones. If you never lived to make it yourself, at least it was gratifying to know that some of your friends would survive. As for the Pro's, I had little interest in shaking their hands although it was good to see some of them leave, if for no other reason than I would no longer have to look at their mugs or watch them bow and scrape to the Chinese.

A group of POW buddies at Camp Five on July 27, 1953—just after we were told we were going home. (I'm in the front row on the far right, wearing a white shirt.)

Once this excitement was over, things settled back to normal in Camp Five, and our daily routine remained unbroken by anything more spectacular than somebody having a birthday and getting thrown into the Yalu River, which had become our custom in Camp Five. One of the more foolish and light-hearted things we did was hold a parade one evening after roll call. A couple of the company clowns, who were always thinking up crazy stunts, decided to hold a mock military funeral. They had one of the boys lie down across a Chinese wheelbarrow, which consisted of two long poles and a burlap bag with a man on each end. They then got a couple of guys carrying wooden sticks for rifles to head the parade. Behind them came several others using twigs for imaginary flutes followed by the Chinese wheelbarrow with this guy all covered up except for his big feet sticking out. At the end of the procession marched the mourners with hats off and sporting very sad faces. As the parade marched around the company area, others joined until the procession included

nearly everybody in our company. By this time the Chinese were standing around with their mouths open and wondering what the deuce was
going on. Finally, someone either told them or they figured it out, and
they broke up our little military funeral. Such events relieved the monotony of prison life and helped us from feeling too sorry for ourselves,
as well as giving everybody but the Chinese a good laugh.

In May of 1953 something nice happened. The Chinese floated a bunch
of big logs down the Yalu to Camp Five. We carried the logs up the hill
to First Company where a makeshift sawmill was set up, and the logs
were cut down into two-by-twos. We carried these two-by-twos back
to the various companies where volunteer "carpenters" cut them into
lengths for double-decker beds. The Chinese then issued us rope that
we twined in such a way that it held the beds together and became our
springs. After all those months of sleeping on the floor, we finally had
our own bunks. This improved our living conditions at least 100 percent, and, almost immediately, our kidneys began operating in a more
normal fashion.

In June we had a big sports event in Camp Five. The different companies held competitions in basketball, softball, soccer, volleyball, and
track and field events. There were also swimming races and a diving
exhibition on the Yalu. It was quite an affair and lasted almost two weeks.
The Chinese took many photographs that they later used for propaganda purposes.

Shortly thereafter, it began to rain and it kept right on raining. The
Yalu River kept rising and soon overflowed the sea wall and the large
parade field that we had so painfully constructed the summer before.
The floodwaters had just about disappeared when on July 27 we heard
the most unbelievable news of all. Our moment had finally arrived,
just hours after the signing of the cease-fire! We were told that within
one hour we would all fall out. Nobody knew for sure what was going
to happen, but rumors were flying fast and furious. We noticed that
throughout the camp there were little groups of Chinese standing
around. Some of them were photographers so we figured whatever was
about to happen must be big news. The Chinese were very glum and

not saying anything. When the bell rang, we assembled in record time. The "Screaming Skull" was standing out front with a paper of some kind in his hand. He began slowly to talk and then suddenly, in a louder and louder voice to drown out our chattering voices, he blurted out the news we wanted so desperately to hear. The cease-fire had been signed. Some of the men laughed, some cried, some jumped up and down, some began to shake their neighbor's hand, some fainted, and a few actually cracked up and went to pieces. It was quite a time in old Camp Five. The news was hard to believe, but surely it must be true. The hours that followed were the happiest of our lives. We gathered into little groups, talked and laughed, and speculated on how soon would come our actual release. We asked each other how we would get to Panmunjom and then on home. We talked about what we would do first, how we would spend all that back pay, and all the good things we would eat. That night, for the first time in the history of Camp Five, no one was interested in food, going to sleep, or doing anything but just talking about this glorious news. A few of us also gathered together and thanked the good Lord for His goodness and mercy.

The following day we had more good news. We learned that Camp Five was going to be the first of the non-Korean POW camps to be cleared. This was followed by the announcement that the camp would be cleared in two groups. This meant there would not be much more waiting. The next day the Chinese announced the first list of men to be repatriated. I kept listening and hoping, but my name was not called with the first group. Those of us in the second group began worrying we might be left behind. On August 1 or 2, we watched the first group load onto the barges that would take them forever away from Camp Five. I wondered if I would ever see them again—and many I did not, including some who had been my closest friends. Of course, there were others I would not miss at all. The rest of that day seemed very quiet, and I kept wondering where the first men were on their journey home.

The next day the Chinese announced that the second and final group would leave on August 5. They also announced that the first prisoner exchange would begin on the same day. The three days of waiting for the calling of the second list were the longest of my life. I tried to sleep a little, but the excitement was just too much, and the suspense was killing me. It was an unforgettable moment when my name was finally called.

About this time, I first heard that some of the Pro's were refusing repatriation and were not going home. I think seven of the twenty-one were at one time in Camp Five. I knew five of these turncoats in Camp Five: H. G. Adams, O. G. Bell, R. E. Douglas, S. D. Hawkins, and L. D. Skinner. After the war I was called to testify about their activities by the Counter Intelligence Corps (see Appendix, document 6).

At the time, the news of their defection was quite a shock, and I thought they were really off their rocker. It was hard to comprehend even for those of us who had known some of them to understand why they would want to do such a thing. But there seemed to be several reasons why. They were afraid to go home with those of us who had been wronged by them. They also feared the charges they would surely have to face back home. Some of them really believed in what they were doing and that the Chinese and the whole Communist world would treat them like kings and heroes. It was the culmination and climax of the lives of betrayal that they had been living these past few years. It was impossible not to feel a little sorry for them, but the ones who really deserved our sympathy were their parents and loved ones who would have to face hardships that American mothers never before had to bear. How these men could do such a thing to their parents was more than anyone could understand. It was a sad situation and one that caused the rest of us deep and lasting pain, hardship, and shame. After returning to the States, people would often ask us *why, why, why* these men had refused to come home.

The day I left Pyoktong behind seemed like the beginning of the end to a long bad dream. The last night in Camp Five no one got much sleep. Early the next morning all bedding and extra clothing were put in a big pile outside the warehouse. The cooks had been up all night baking bread and packing canned pork for the trip, but at a time like this who was interested in food? Each of us was allowed to take one complete change of clothing and whatever personal items he might still have. Before leaving Pyoktong that morning, the Chinese carefully went over our personal belongings and conducted a complete shakedown for anything they didn't want to leave camp. Evidently they didn't want any of those poems or diaries that might still be in circulation to leave camp. They were also looking for lists of the names of prisoners who had died.

It was almost noon when we finally boarded the barges and slowly pulled away from the peninsula that had been P. U. (Pyoktong University; also, "smells bad") for so long. As the barges swung slowly around the point, I looked for the last time at Pyoktong, now almost a deserted village. It looked so quiet and ghostlike that morning. Tears came to my eyes, especially when I looked across the water to the valley and the hills beyond where countless hundreds of Americans lay buried in shallow, unmarked graves. For them there would be no repatriation.

The barge took us just a mile or so to the landing where a big convoy of trucks waited. The truck I was assigned to did not take us very far. About four or five miles out of Pyoktong, the tie rod broke and the truck careened into the side of the mountain. This shook us up, but no one was hurt. In fact, we were relieved not to have gone over the cliff on the other side of the road, which was a sheer drop of several hundred feet. Once again I thanked my Maker for His protection. The Chinese then loaded us on the last truck in the convoy, which was a spare. The road took us to Sinuiju, the city on the west coast where the Yalu River runs into the China Sea. It was a scary trip. We traveled over some of the highest mountains in Korea, and after having been grounded for so long, driving twenty miles an hour seemed like we were flying. Our young Chinese driver thought he was a jet pilot instead of a truck driver. He would breeze around those hairpin curves, blowing his horn only after he was well around them. On one occasion we narrowly missed a head-on collision with a truck filled with gas drums. In that six-hour ride, our truck actually sideswiped six other trucks, killed one chicken, and hit an old Korean carrying a huge load of brush on his back.

In Sinuiju we were crammed into a string of boxcars with just enough room for us to sit down. This was to be our home for three long nights and two long days. We got away shortly after dark and rolled along in sort of a lunge-and-coast fashion for about an hour. Then we stopped for some unknown reason for at least another hour. That night, however, we

made better time than during any other part of the trip, perhaps because the tracks in the north were in better repair than further south.
Whatever the reason, it was a slow ride. The next day we had a welcome break beside a fast flowing, cool mountain stream where we were
allowed to go swimming. We noticed that we had made very little
progress during the daylight hours, probably because the Chinese did
not want us to see any more of this territory than could be helped.

Each boxcar had its own Chinese instructor and its own chow. The
days were extremely hot and dragged by so slowly that I wondered if
we would ever get off this vermin-infested train. On the second night
and day we made even less progress. In the early afternoon we reached
Pyongyang. I had thought the city was in terrible shape back in 1951,
but now there was hardly a building still intact. We got off the train and
were loaded once again onto trucks. The railroad bridge across the
Pyongyang River was in such dangerous shape that the train inched
across it empty while our trucks drove across another bridge. On the
other side we again piled into the boxcars.

Not far south of Pyongyang was a rest stop set up for returning prisoners. Here we could wash up, stretch out on bamboo mats underneath
a huge shelter, and get a little rest. We were also given some rice and
beans to eat. We spent about three hours here before once again getting
back on the boxcars—for the very last time. It was almost dark when the
train pulled out of the rest station and proceeded south to Kaesong. That
night one of the men in the last car, who was evidently experiencing severe mental problems, jumped from the train and went rolling down the
bank. The Chinese halted the train, and sent back a couple of guards to
look for him. The train, however, did not wait for them to return. The
next day they brought this poor fellow into Kaesong by truck.

After arriving in Kaesong about three o'clock in the morning, we
were loaded on trucks for a three- or four-mile ride to what would be
our last stop before freedom. The date was August 8, 1953. This repatriation camp had the nicest building I stayed in during my long captivity in Korea. It was an old botanical college and was still reasonably
clean and respectable looking. Outside of the bedbugs that were as big
as the nail on my little finger, it was not at all bad. Some of the guys

who had left in the first group from Camp Five were still there, although they were getting ready to leave that morning for Panmunjom, which was only thirty miles away. About one hundred and fifty U.N. prisoners a day were being repatriated at Panmunjom and about twice that number of South Koreans. The South Koreans were kept segregated from the U.N. prisoners.

The repatriation process worked something like this. Each morning about 4:00 or 4:30, the Chinese would come around and call off the names of the men to be repatriated that day. These men would be taken over for an early breakfast, a shakedown, and then divided into three groups. The first group would leave the camp about 8:00, the second at 9:00, and the last at 10:00. One hour after leaving, they would once again be free men. Those left behind would bid the men goodbye and go back to bed. For the first time the daily routine in camp was left up to us prisoners. There were two meals served per day, plus a noontime snack. For breakfast there was rice and beans and maybe sliced tomatoes or something extra. For noon there was fried bread and tea. The evening meal was usually steamed bread, rice, and pork. About the second or third day the Red Cross brought over some American soap, toothpaste, and cigarettes. It was the first time the Red Cross had been able to reach us. These stateside products were like something from heaven.

Each morning was filled with the terrible suspense of listening to the names being called for that day's repatriation. I breathlessly waited and listened for my name. It seemed like I was always standing there waving goodbye to someone else and watching them get on trucks and ride out to freedom. Finally, on the morning of August 12, with only a few of us left from Camp Five, my name was called.

Thus began the day I had been dreaming about for more than twenty-two months. I watched the first group load into the waiting trucks and waved goodbye. Another hour dragged by, and the second group loaded up, and once more I was there waving. The next hour seemed much longer. The trucks finally returned, and the Chinese motioned for our bunch to load up. As we rolled down the road to freedom, it seemed so unreal and unnatural to be spending my last few minutes as a prisoner of war. The truck finally stopped at a barricade. I waited nervously while the minutes ticked away. Finally, the barricade was rolled away, and we moved forward to the exchange point. The Chinese officer got out and was met by an American officer. Both had rosters in their hands, and one by one our names were called off. First the Chinese read my name; then the American did. I stepped down off the truck and was quickly escorted a few steps to an army tent. As I walked across that line of freedom and entered the tent, another American officer shook my hand and said, "Welcome home, soldier." I was a free man, and my eyes filled with tears. At the other end of the tent another American officer handed me a brown manila envelope. I was then escorted to a waiting ambulance that transported me to this dream world called Freedom Village. It was too wonderful and emotional an experience ever to put into words.

Freedom Village was a tremendous place for us. All the personnel treated us royally. As I stepped out of the ambulance, General Maxwell Taylor was there to greet us. Once inside another big tent, my return processing started. I had forgotten how fast the army could move, and so much happened in the next three hours that my head was swimming. After a few preliminary checks, I was taken to a section set aside as a chapel. There were chaplains there to administer to my long neglected religious rites, which was certainly one of my biggest thrills.

From there I was taken to tables where I could choose whatever I wanted for a snack. To taste ice cream again was wonderful. Next the Red Cross gave each of us a little bag complete with toilet articles. Across the street was another big tent with showers. I tossed my summer blues and Chinese underwear into a big bin. That first shower was an unimaginable pleasure. From there I went into an adjoining room where I was given a big towel, a hospital robe, and slippers. Next came the medical station and a complete physical. This also included a shot in the arm, which convinced me that I was back in the hands of the U.S. Army! On down the line was a mail call section where our most recent letters from home and loved ones were waiting. Then I was permitted to lie down on a hospital bed and read my mail. The nurses brought trays full of the most delicious food I had tasted since leaving home. From there I went across to supply where I got a new set of fatigues, underwear, socks, handkerchiefs, caps, and shoes. To get back into army

A Red Cross volunteer took this photograph of
me at Freedom Village, South Korea, on August
12, 1953, the day of my release from Camp Five.

clothes again was a great feeling. I moved next to a lounge with soft
music, magazines, comfortable chairs, and nice-looking girls to bring
refreshments. After a short while, my name was called, and I was loaded
into an army four-by-four and driven to the heliport on a hill back of
Freedom Village. I was flown by helicopter to Inchon, South Korea. Many
of my friends and buddies were there to greet and welcome me back to
freedom. Then, a new Chevrolet command car drove me to a post for
further processing before boarding a ship for home.

My processing ended with me drawing about two hundred dollars
in military script for back pay. I was assigned a bunk and then it was
time for a wonderful supper, complete with a big vitamin capsule. That
evening there was a good American movie and then refreshments were
passed out at the snack bar. This was really living. That night for the
first time since I left Japan, I slept on a mattress between two nice clean
sheets with a real pillow.

Home at last! The uss *General Hase* docked at San Francisco on August 29, 1953. (I'm in the front row, sixth from the left.)

The next day I was issued more clothing and had a chance to go to the special post exchange where I bought a wristwatch to replace the one I had tossed over the side of the mountain when I was captured. I also bought a camera and film, some extra underwear, a wallet, stationery, and lots of other things, including souvenirs to send home. The Red Cross took my picture and, along with a cablegram, sent it home to my parents. Yes sir, I was really living. Again there was a good movie and more refreshments. There were also chapel programs, and it was wonderful to sing some of those old hymns again. The next day was similar with more processing and more entertainment. The following day we climbed aboard big army busses while being serenaded by a military band and rode down to the pier where we once more boarded a landing craft, only this time the landing craft took us off the rock which had been my domicile for two long, hard years. As we pulled away from the shore, for the first time Korea looked beautiful.

Our ship was the *General Hase,* one of the largest of the army transports. Once aboard we were permitted to send another cablegram home. The ship waited in the harbor for two days until a bunch of ex-pows

At home in Jupiter, Florida, before my October 1953 discharge.

were brought aboard from Camp One. There were also rotating troops on board, which gave us a full load.

Our processing continued on board ship, but I had plenty of time to catch up on the news of what had been going on in the outside world those past two years. As former POWs, we had several special privileges aboard ship such as our own sun deck, late breakfast, first in line for lunch and supper, first to see the movies, and no pulling of details except keeping our own bunk and gear picked up and out of the way.

After a few days at sea, some old scores were settled in mob fashion. There was a Kangaroo Court, and some of those accused of collaborating with or squealing to the Chinese or of having done something to receive special treatment ended up in the ship's hospital. One incident took place right below my top bunk. About four or five guys almost killed another ex-POW. The MPs arrived and broke it up and took the guy to sick bay, and there were similar attacks on other parts of the ship.

Ours was the second ship to dock in San Francisco with ex-POWs on board. This was also an occasion that I would never forget. The military band was there, as well as parents, relatives, and close friends. This was once more the good old United States. It was wonderful to see so many happy people and even more wonderful to have friends and relatives to greet me. Home was now only a matter of hours away. After some additional quick processing, I was safely aboard a big four-engine plane and heading east. Everyone had been so good to me since my release, but what would it be like when I reached home the next day? It was all that I had ever dreamed of and more!

In spite of my obvious happiness, there were still those haunting thoughts. I knew I was one of the lucky ones. I had made it home, I had my life ahead of me, and I seemed in fairly good health, compared to many of my friends. I knew I had so very, very much for which to be thankful. But what about those who were not so fortunate? What about those who had lost limbs, or those who would be forever confined to hospital beds, or those who would never return? Will we ever know what happened to those 8,176 men who remain unaccounted for—the MIAS—many of whom were certainly POWs?

The North Korean wind still blows cold over the remains of thousands of American servicemen who died on those forgotten battlefields or in despised captivity.

Let the word of Christ dwell in you richly in all wisdom; teaching and admonishing one another in psalms and hymns and spiritual songs, singing with grace in your hearts to the Lord.
    —*Colossians 3:16*

Epilogue: 2001—Fifty Years Later

Lo, I am with you always.
—*Matthew 28:20*

Today, it seems as if my return home was a confused dream. If being free was a dream, I didn't want to awaken. I had never experienced such a feeling of euphoria during my first twenty-five years; yet, all was not well. I remember telling a reporter that I felt like a millionaire and that my troubles were all over. Not true! Of course, I had no idea how a millionaire should feel; as a matter of fact, fifty years later, I still don't. Even at the moment of my release, I felt a certain numbness of mind and body, a feeling that still exists. At the time, I had no idea that such a malady had a name. Today, we know it as Post-Traumatic Stress Disorder (PTSD), an affliction that we first publicly associated with Vietnam veterans. In my case, PTSD was the result of combat, captivity, release, and rehabilitation, all of which were very traumatic for me.

I brought home from combat and the POW experience not only PTSD but a severe loss of hearing, chronic dysentery, anxiety disorder, irritable bowel syndrome, nutritional deficiencies, traumatic arthritis, helminthiasis (infectious residuals from parasitic worms), frostbite, and peripheral neuropathy (a neurological disorder characterized by burning and tingling of the extremities). The doctors on board the ship coming home recorded that I had nerve damage, chronic dysentery, and a loss of hearing. In 1954, I went to the VA Hospital in Miami for these service-related ailments. The doctors there granted me 10 percent disability for my nerves, 20 percent for the dysentery, but 0 percent for my

85

loss of hearing. After a couple of years, they called me back for another examination and asked how I was feeling. Because I was still so glad to be home, and because I didn't want to have anything more to do with the military or even to think about my POW experiences, I foolishly told them I felt okay. So they cut me to 20 percent. Then, in 1962, I was pushed back to 0 percent disability where I remained until after my PTSD breakdown in 1978.

I did go to an eye, nose, ear, and throat specialist when I got home. He pumped this stuff out of my ear canals, just globs and globs of gook—that's the only way I can describe it. The doctor told me every time I could think of it to hold both my nostrils, blow, and put pressure on my ears and that gradually my hearing should improve. But my hearing only got worse. When I began teaching, I had great difficulty in the classroom. If the kids asked me a question, I answered what I thought they asked, but it often wasn't the right question. They would laugh. I tried to keep my sense of humor, but it was difficult.

Finally, at the big protocol exam of, I think, 1982 or 1983, I was bumped up to 40 percent disability for PTSD and given an extra 10 percent for my loss of hearing. I appealed this decision, and after a couple of years it rose to 60 percent. I later received another 10 percent for irritable bowel syndrome, which supposedly covered the lingering effects of my dysentery. VA regulations state that once you are at 70 percent disability, with more than 40 percent for one area, you are considered unemployable, and you qualify for 100 percent disability. I appealed my claims several times. In 1996 I was awarded 100 percent disability retroactive to July 1, 1994. Of course, it took four decades of dealing with the VA to get this compensation rating. When I was finally awarded 100 percent disability, I was sixty-eight years old. Doctors figure that every year in an Asian POW camp knocks five years off your life, so I was already living on borrowed time.

In retrospect, I now know that I had become very withdrawn and introverted during my incarceration, and this behavior continued after my return to the States. I did try to put down my memories during the sixty-day convalescence leave the army granted me before my discharge. But after I finished my narrative, I tried to blank out everything about my Korean War experiences. I did not talk about Korea with my family or friends unless they asked a direct question. Even then they realized from my abrupt reply that I didn't want to talk about the war.

I did take advantage of the GI Bill and resumed my college education. I had completed three semesters before the war, and now I wanted to finish, but because of my health, this was to be very difficult. I had hoped being a student would not only occupy my time but also help my long-term rehabilitation. The problem was I could scarcely function. I was very nervous. I had the residuals of dysentery. What I was eating would either immediately go out my bowels or back up through my throat. I almost totally withdrew within myself. I dreaded being in class for fear I would have a sick spell or soil my clothes, and I didn't want to talk to anyone. I would go days at a time and not say a word to anybody. I marvel today that I only missed one class in three years, and that was because my car broke down.

I met my future wife, Valdeen Banks, while attending Palm Beach Junior College. We both transferred to Florida State University where we started dating. After we graduated in the field of education, we were married in April of 1957. She tried to bring me out of my social shell, but to this day we have never really talked about my combat and POW experiences.

After we married, Valdeen began teaching, but I did not because of my ongoing health problems. Instead, I worked for three years in Jupiter, Florida, with my father in the nursery business and for my brother, who was a contractor, as a bookkeeper and payroll clerk. We then moved to Gainesville where I took two semesters of accounting. I was hired as the assistant accountant for the Florida School for the Deaf and Blind in St. Augustine where I worked for the next four and a half years. We also adopted two infant sons, twenty-two months apart.

In 1964 my medical and social problems were still with me, and I continued to feel overly anxious about everything, but I made myself begin teaching. I ended up at St. Augustine High School where I taught history until I retired in 1989. I also completed a master's degree in 1971. Very few of our school or church friends knew anything about my POW experiences because until 1978 I did not talk about them.

Richard M. and Valdeen Bassett, 1984.

In spite of my academic success, a good teaching position, professional and church friends, and a family, I was badly in need of help.
One Friday in April 1978, I came home from school and, without any
goodbyes, got in the car and drove away from family and friends without having any plans of ever seeing any of them again—at least in this
world. What happened? I was suffering a complete breakdown. Without any outward warning, it was PTSD, and in full force. There had been
tensions in our marriage, largely due to a lack of communication on my
part, not only about the war and how I was feeling, but also on all family matters. We had suffered several deaths in our families, and my wife
and I were often the main caregivers, which also was very stressful.

But God is good! I did not drive into a tree or a canal that day. Instead, I drove to the VA Hospital in Gainesville where I spent the next
eighty-eight days in the psychiatric ward. There were some real basket
cases there, but the staff was very compassionate and divided us into
smaller groups. This meant I was pretty well matched up with others
suffering the same kinds of problems. I was finally persuaded that I

At my desk in St. Augustine High School, 1980.

had to talk about my war experiences. I had to admit to family, friends, students at school, and, above all, to myself that all this had really happened to me—that it was an integral part of my personal history. I also had to assess and seek closure on certain events that had occurred during the twenty-five years between August of 1953, when I gained my freedom, and 1978, when I suffered my breakdown. My wife has been very supportive of me in our forty-five years of marriage.

I had been carrying a great deal of guilt over surviving combat and becoming a POW. I had spent literally hundreds of hours (usually after awakening from a nightmare about combat or captivity) pondering what I could have done differently. I still cannot resolve this problem in my dreams because, after almost half a century, I still suffer nightmares and flashbacks. The good news now is that I can usually roll over and go back to sleep.

The day I was released I remember walking down a path in Freedom Village. I met an officer and promptly saluted. He did not return my salute. I thought to myself, "Oh, yeah, one does not salute in combat." But we were not then in combat. Could his refusal to salute have been the first indication that my loyalty was suspect? Coming home aboard ship, we were regarded with suspicion by some of our military interrogators who wondered if we had collaborated with the enemy. And this did not stop after arriving home. For the next seven or eight years, the FBI intermittently questioned me and many other former POWs. These agents asked me about other POWs rather than about myself. They were friendly enough, but I realized they were also asking other former prisoners about me. It was terrible. We were all under suspicion. It was the Cold War, the legacy of McCarthyism was still alive, and there were all those negative reports in the press questioning our loyalty. Even after I moved to Saint Augustine in 1960, the FBI still called on me.

After reading an article in the *Ex-POW Bulletin* concerning the Freedom of Information Act, I requested and obtained my government records. I had quite a file. There were some one hundred pages in all, and they included interviews the FBI had conducted with other former prisoners about me. Only one said I had cooperated with the Chinese. His evidence was that I had given book reports. Fortunately, nothing came of this, and on the last page the report declared me a loyal American citizen!

There were many other incidents that bothered me. Shortly after I was discharged, an older man, who had never served in the military, asked me, "How come you didn't stay over there with the Turncoats?" On another occasion a VA psychiatrist asked me, "How were things in the rest camp on the Yalu River?" In the early 1980s I was driving a car in the Veterans Day Parade. We were all decked out with flags and identifying signs. As we slowly drove by, I overheard a long-haired, barefoot young man say to his girlfriend, "All you have to do is give up and ride in parades the rest of your life." Needless to say, that was my first and last parade. To this day the general public is ignorant about the degradation and horror of being a POW. It equates the POW experience with *Hogan's Heroes* and combat with John Wayne. In combat and captivity your life expectancy is measured in split seconds, and in no way does the media or the public understand that those of us who have been there relive these terrifying moments daily for the rest of our lives.

At the 1988 Christmas party for the former POWS in the Florida First Coast American Ex-Prisoner of War chapter. Holding the other end of the flag is Ed Creamer *(left)*, a POW in Japan during WWII.

In response to a 1996 *Florida-Times Union* article based on a poll of Americans, entitled "Magical '50s—An Ideal Time," I wrote the following letter to the editor:

> Evidently the pollsters never talked to any Korean War veterans (1950–1953) or their loved ones. Over 1.5 million Americans fought in bloody Korea. Especially they didn't poll the loved ones of those 54,246 killed between 1950–1953 or the over 3,700 who died as POWS. Certainly they didn't talk to any POWS who somehow lived through captivity (only half of us are still alive); or to the 103,284 who were wounded in combat, many still in veterans hospitals; or to the loved ones of 8,100 still listed as MIA (missing in action).

The Forgotten War in Korea is only remembered by a few, is forgotten by most, and is just barely mentioned in our classrooms today. It was hardly an "Ideal Time" for us or our loved ones. But then these facts would distract from the theme of the "Magical '50s."

The healing process is so very slow and is never really completed. There are, however, things we former prisoners can do to help ourselves. At the Veterans Affairs Out-Patient Clinic (VAOPC) in Jacksonville, we have an XPOW support group. Most of the men are from World War II. Until a few years ago we even had one from World War I. Three of us are from Korea and one from Vietnam. I find these meetings to be good therapy, and I try to attend the meetings at least once a month now that I'm retired. As often as possible, I also attend the annual reunions of the Korean War POWs, the 25th Infantry Division, and the 14th Infantry Regiment. A few years ago I even met the fellow who was my replacement in the 14th after I got captured. The camaraderie is great. After all, only those who were there can truly understand what we all have gone through. Staying as active as time and health permit is also important. I wear a number of hats in my church, including Sunday School director; I serve as a mentor at St. Augustine High School in a program called Take Stock in Children; I participate in the Retired Senior Volunteer Program, which, among other activities, helps elementary children with their reading; and I give talks to school and civic groups about the Korean War. Along with travel, church, and grandchildren, such activities help keep my mind and body occupied.

I am neither a hero nor a coward, just a survivor. As I look back, I have to admit that in many respects, my life after repatriation has certainly not been all I dreamed of during those long, endless nights in North Korea when that cold Manchurian wind blew over Camp Five. I do, however, continue to believe in priorities such as God, family, and country. From my heart I can say if my country called and I were able, I would again be willing to serve. At the same time I pray that my grandchildren will not have to fight a war. I do not hate the Chinese. They believed what they were told. Most of them had no other choice. I don't have any hatred for anyone. To me, being a citizen of this great land is a high privilege. I appreciate those who willingly serve as military peacekeepers all over the world, for I understand better than most that being a soldier can fundamentally change or even cost one his life. Above all, I believe we are a nation blessed by God and that we should live by our creed, "In God We Trust." One of my favorite Bible verses says it all: "If God be for us, who can stand against us?" (Romans 8:31).

Appendix

The United States government's investigations of former Korean War POWs began almost immediately upon liberation, and they continued on board the ships carrying the men home. Interrogating officers asked each former prisoner if he had seen instances of collaboration and if he knew anything about those twenty-one men who chose to defect. The officer then made a recommendation about whether or not further questioning was necessary. After arriving in the States, some of these men were singled out for immediate investigation, whereas others were pestered for years by various government agencies seeking additional information.

These investigations sought to uncover alleged prisoner misbehavior and collaboration; but, in reality, they reflected the continuing tensions and paranoia of the Cold War. After all, former prisoners of other twentieth-century wars did not suffer such indignities. To be sure, twenty-one Americans did refuse repatriation, choosing instead to stay behind in the People's Republic of China. But this was only twenty-one of more than 7,000 prisoners. Nevertheless, an entire generation of young men came under suspicion, and Richard Bassett was no exception.

It is difficult to define "collaboration" or "giving aid to the enemy." The most egregious form occurred when a prisoner jeopardized the health and welfare of his fellow prisoners by cooperating with his captors. In Korea, these "Rats" made up less than 5 percent of the POW population. Lesser charges included communicating with the enemy beyond allowable name, rank, and serial number; cooperating with the enemy to obtain much-needed food and medicine; using the prison library; signing peace petitions; writing letters that contained positive statements about their incarceration; writing book reviews; and admitting acquaintance with any of the notorious twenty-one defectors. Such investigations encouraged hearsay evidence, and all too often they afforded disgruntled prisoners the chance to take out frustrations and grudges on their fellow prisoners.

Under the Freedom of Information Act, Richard Bassett obtained his official file, the major parts of which appear in this appendix. Although Bassett was eventually exonerated of any wrongdoing, he, like his fellow prisoners, nevertheless had to suffer the humiliation of suspicion.

DOCUMENT 1

In signing this certificate at the Inchon Replacement Depot, on August 13, 1953, Richard Bassett promised not to disclose any information about his incarceration, but the statute of limitations on such promises has long expired.

C E R T I F I C A T E

I certify that I have read and fully understand all the provisions of Circular 131, Headquarters, United States Army Forces, Far East, 1953, subject: Disclosure of Information in Connection With Personnel Escaped, Liberated, or Repatriated From a Hostile Force, to Include Evaders of Capture in Enemy or Enemy-Occupied Territory and Internees in Neutral Countries, and will at all times hereafter comply fully therewith.

I understand that disclosure of military information to unauthorized persons will make me liable to disciplinary action.

I realize that it is my duty during my military service, and later as a civilian, to take all possible precautions to prevent disclosure, by word of mouth or otherwise, of military information of this nature.

Name (Print)___Richard M. Bassett___Signed

Grade____Cpl____SN_US 1420606_/ Dated_13 Aug 1953___Place_Inchon Repl Depot

Unit___8057th Army Unit APO 971_____Witness

58

38-3-Army-AG Admin Cen-AFFE-25M

DOCUMENT 2

The interviewing officer at the Inchon Replacement Depot, Lt. H. K. Danielson, wrote the following description of Richard Bassett.

DOCUMENT TWO

CONFIDENTIAL

7930 - Psych Obs. (No disease Found) ~~SECRET~~ Interview - 13 Aug 53

This 25 year-old single white male cpl with 29 months service comes from a semi-rural Florida town and his parents are lower middle socio-economic class. He finished high school and one year of college before entering the Army. He planned to enter horticulture, his father's field, but now feels that he will enter the religious field which is directly related to his prison experience.

This soldier was captured when ambushed on patrol five miles in front of his unit outpost in late 1951. He feels that he received good treatment at the hands of his captors, compared to what was told to him of incidents early in others confinement. Strong religious feeling prompted him to organize daily and Sunday religious meetings, but he is quick to deny credit, and adopts a modest attitude when questioned in this regard. When the group instructors (Chinese) attempted to use harassing tactics to annoy them as well as to throw suspicion on them, they resisted mainly, it seems, because of the persistence of this soldier. He says that when they told them that they could not hold religious meetings and that religion was a medium to control poor people, this soldier told them that in the lectures against religion in the "new democracies" that complete religious freedom existed "which put them on the spot,"and they had to let us meet. Typical tactics used to harass them included shining flashlights into their faces as they sat in a group and making fun of them. The soldier describes a strong empathic relationship with his mother who isvery religious. Present plans include attending a Bible school to become a Bible teacher.

Mental status: This placid soldier of above average intelligence focusses on his use of religion to hold himself together during his prison camp experiences. He speaks coherently and logically, with emphasis on his methods to push his religious feelings. However, he is modest and denies anything more than a secondary role in the formation of the religious group in the camp. However, he seems to have an adequate grasp of reality and maintains a flexible and spontaneous outlook at the present time. Because of the channelization of his energies he says he never became bored or lost interest while in camp.

H. K. DANIELSON
1/Lt   MC

57

BASSETT, RICHARD A.   ~~SECRET~~   US 14206061   Line No. 287

~~SECURITY INFORMATION~~

CONFIDENTIAL

0021

DOCUMENT 3

The first phase of questioning of returning POWs took place on the USS *W. F. Hase* on August 24, 1953. The concluding comments read: "Returnee apparently did not engage in 'Progressive' activities in PW camp and it is the opinion of the undersigned that returnee is an extremely religious person in that he was persistent enough to carry on religious work throughout his captivity. Not believed to be a Security Risk as he does not appear to have absorbed but very little of communist doctrine."

PHASE I QUESTIONNAIRE FOR RECOVERED U.N. PsW

Place _At Sea, Aboard U.S.N.S. Gen. Hase_ Date _24 Aug 53_

Name _BASSETT_ (Last) _Richard_ (First) _M._ (MI)

Branch of Service _Inf_

Rank _Corporal_ SN _US 14326061_ Age _25_ Race _Caucasian_

Organization (When captured) _25th_ (Div) _14th_ (Regt) _3d_ (Bn) _"I"_ (Co)

Representative of what UNC force _American_

Years Education _1½ College_ Duty when captured _Ass't BAR rifleman_

Nationality (American, Colombian, etc.) _American_

Place and date of capture & designation of capturing unit _Near Kumhwa, 6 Oct 51_
Unit designation unknown (CCF)

Circumstances of capture, viz, wounded, separate from unit, etc. _Out on patrol, six (6)_
men passed an ambush & were Cut off from rest of patrol, 4 captured, including returnee

Place and date of release _Panmunjom, Korea, 12 Aug 53_

Principal place (places) of internment:

Pyuktong, Camp #5, Co. #3 (Place)   _2 Nov 51 - 5 Aug 53_ (Date)   _Plot Reported for wall news paper, non-political activities within platoon. Engaged in Religious work with PWs._ (Duties)

_____ (Place)   _____ (Date)   _____ (Duties)

_____ (Place)   _____ (Date)   _____ (Duties)

COMMENTS AND RECOMMENDATIONS OF PHASE II INTERROGATOR

Returnee apparently did not engage in "Progressive" activities in PW camp and
it is the opinion of the undersigned that returnee is an extremely
religious person in that he was persistant enough to carry on religious
work throughout his captivity. Not believed to be a Security Risk as he
does not appear to have absorbed but
[   ] of communist doctrine. 53

(Signature, rank and organization)

0023

Appendix

DOCUMENT 4

Richard Bassett signed the following statement declaring that all his
previous statements were freely given. Interrogating officer Don Hall
explained that Bassett was not coerced or promised immunity for his
statements.

'I further state that the foregoing statement was made by me freely and voluntarily, and without promise of benefit, or threat or use of force or duress. I have read the foregoing statement consisting of __two__ pages, and it is true and correct to the best of my knowledge and belief._____

Richard M Bassett

Richard M. Bassett, Cpl, US14206061

Sworn and subscribed to before me this __24th__ day of __August 1953__ at

(a) _____, or

(b) sea aboard the __USNS GEN W. F. HASE__ .

PAUL R. ASHMORE, CAPT, INF

SUMMARY COURT

We hereby certify that we were present at

(a) _____, or

(b) sea aboard the __USNS GEN W. F. HASE__ .

when __Richard M Bassett__ made the above statement and that he was fully advised of his rights as set forth above, that no promise of immunity or reward was made to him, that no force or duress was used or threatened, and that the above statement was freely and voluntarily made. We further certify that the said __Richard M.__

__Bassett__ signed the above statement in our presence.

WITNESSED: Don Hall 106 Plant City, Fla.

page __two__ of __two__ pages

0026

DOCUMENT 5

On August 26, 1953, Col. John B. McKean declared that additional interrogations are necessary "to determine in all finality [Richard Bassett's] essential loyalty."

287

TAB 11 (Form Letter #1)
to Administrative Inclosure
For JIPB SOP

HEADQUARTERS
UNITED STATES ARMY FORCES, FAR EAST (ADV)
JOINT INTELLIGENCE PROCESSING BOARD
APO 500

26 August 1953

SUBJECT: BASSETT, Richard M Cpl
US14206061

TO: Assistant Chief of Staff, G-2
             Department of the Army
             Washington 25, D. C.

1. A review of results of the detailed Counterintelligence interrogation, AFFE CIC files, and an examination of the results of interrogation of other repatriated US personnel fails to indicate at this time
that subject has additional information of intelligence value.

2. Based upon information presently available to this Board it
is therefore recommended that subject be cleared for such additional
disposition as may be directed.

3. However, if circumstances permit, exploitation in the Zone of
the Interior may reveal information not obtained in this limited processing. Due to the limited time subject was available for interrogation,
it was not possible to determine in all finality his essential loyalty,
nor to obtain full intelligence information.

For the Joint Intelligence Processing Board:

JOHN B. McKEAN
Lt Col   Inf
Chairman

54

0016

DOCUMENT 6

Richard Bassett's interrogation resumed on June 29, 1955, in Jupiter, Florida.

AGENT REPORT
(SR 380-320-10)

1. NAME OF SUBJECT OR TITLE OF INCIDENT	2. DATE SUBMITTED
INTERROGATION OF WITNESS	29 June 1955
	3. CONTROL SYMBOL OR FILE NUMBER
	C80 50117

4. REPORT OF FINDINGS

(INTERROGATION OF WITNESS) On 25 June 1955, Richard Milton Bassett, Student, Florida State University, Tallahassee, Florida, presently living at Route 1, Jupiter, Florida, for the summer vacation, and formerly a Corporal, US 14206061, Infantry, United States Army, was interrogated relative to all twenty-one (21) Volunteer Non-Repatriates (VNR) in accordance with instructions in the "Outline of Interrogation", Military District of Washington, Office of the Assistant Chief of Staff G-2, Washington 25, D. C. The information obtained during this interrogation is included in sworn statements concerning VNR's listed below:

Adams, H. G.	(EXHIBIT_____)
Bell, O. G.	(EXHIBIT_____)
Douglas, R. E.	(EXHIBIT_____)
Hawkins, S. D.	(EXHIBIT_____)
Skinner, L. D.	(EXHIBIT_____)

AGENTS NOTES: Interviewee was cooperative, seemingly truthful, and possessed of above average intelligence. Bassett indicated he had not gone out of his way to associate with Adams, Bell, Douglas, Hawkins, or Skinner, but neither had he tried to avoid them. Source, seemingly a very religious type of person (claiming to have conducted Christmas services in the camp in 1952), at times seemed to be seeking an answer for the aforementioned POWs actions while in the camp. Source appeared to be strongly anti-Communist in belief although he indicated no active resistance to some of the Communist's demands since resistance would have been futile. Bassett's belief seemed to be that the "progressives" should have known a "day of retribution was coming". Source is willing to testify before a court or board concerning his sworn statements.

4

5. TYPED NAME AND ORGANIZATION OF SPECIAL AGENT	6. SIGNATURE OF SPECIAL AGENT
JOHN H. BULLARD, JR., Region VII 111th CIC Detachment	

DA FORM 341 1 APR 52   REPLACES WD AGO FORM 341, 1 JUN 47 WHICH MAY BE USED.

U. S. GOVERNMENT PRINTING OFFICE : 1952 O—998493

DOCUMENT 7

Richard Bassett gave a statement to the Counter Intelligence Corps about Howard G. Adams, one of the twenty-one POWs who refused repatriation.

STATEMENT
(SR 190-45-1)

Explain the nature of the investigation. If deponent is accused or suspected of an offense he must be so informed and this fact affirmatively shown.

PLACE	DATE	FILE NO.
Route No. 1, Jupiter, Florida	29 June 1955	

DEPONENT (Last Name—First Name—Middle Initial)	SERVICE NO.	GRADE
Bassett, Richard M.		

ORGANIZATION (If deponent is a civilian, give address)

TO BE COMPLETED PRIOR TO MAKING STATEMENT

THE ~~~~~~~~~~~~~~~~~~~~~~~~~~~~~~~~~~~~ THE FIFTH AMENDMENT TO THE CONSTITUTION OF THE UNITED STATES) (Strike out only if person making statement IS a member of the Armed Forces) (HAS) (HAVE) BEEN READ TO ME AND MY RIGHTS THEREUNDER HAVE BEEN EXPLAINED TO ME BY **Neil D. Blue, Jr.** WHO INFORMED ME THAT HE IS (A) ~~ **Special Agent** **Military Intelligence** OF THE UNITED STATES (ARMY) ~~~~~~~~~~~~. HE HAS INFORMED ME THAT THIS STATEMENT IS BEING TAKEN IN CONNECTION WITH THE INVESTIGATION OF **Howard-Gayle Adams**

~~~~~~~~~~~~~~~~~~~~ (Strike out words between brackets, if inapplicable). THE FOREGOING HAVING BEEN EXPLAINED TO AND BEING UNDERSTOOD BY ME, I VOLUNTARILY MAKE THE FOLLOWING STATEMENT.

Richard M. Bassett
(SIGNATURE OF DEPONENT)

STATEMENT BEGINS[1]

I, Richard Milton Bassett, Student, Florida State University, Tallahassee, Florida, presently living at Route 1, Jupiter, Florida, for the summer vacation, and formerly a Corporal, US 14 206 061, Infantry, United States Army, was captured on 6 October 1951, near Kumhwa, Korea, and arrived at Camp #5, near Pyoktong, Korea, some time in December 1951. In about January 1952, I, a member of the second platoon, third company, became acquainted with Adams, a member of the fourth platoon, third company, who had arrived at the camp some time prior to myself. I had almost daily contact with Adams until about 5 August 1953, at which time I departed the camp for repatriation. Our association was one of routine acquaintance in which there was no official relationship. Adams was not known to have held any official position in the camp's internal organization. During the entire period of our acquaintanceship, Adams was the Chairman of the Camp Menu Committee, whose duties it was to plan meals and keep a menu posted, but it actually served to keep favored personnel off work details. I did not know how Adams was selected for this position, any specific qualifications he may have possessed, of any coercion that may have been used to get him to accept this position, or of any disadvantage fellow POWs may have incurred from the manner in which he carried out the duties of this position. I have no knowledge of other persons who have direct personal knowledge of Adams' connection with the internal organization of the camp. Adams was a member of the Peace Committee, of a Camp Study Group, and was known to have participated in skits deriding democracy as practiced in America. The purposes of these activities were to further the propaganda efforts of the Chinese Communists and to indoctrinate the other POWs. Adams' qualifications for these activities, his exact degree of participation, or the manner in which he was selected or elected is unknown to me. I believe Adams' participation in these activities was voluntary since he was active in his participation and was not known to have ever offered any resistance to the part he played. I do not believe Adams' participation in these activities had any effect upon those POWs classed by the Chinese Communists as being "reactionaries" but may have served to strengthen the "pro-

EXHIBIT	DEPONENT'S INITIALS	Page 1 of 3 Pages
	RMB	

[1] Additional pages must contain the heading "STATEMENT OF____TAKEN AT____DATED____CONTINUED." The bottom of each additional page must bear the initials of the person making the statement and be identified as "PAGE____OF____PAGES."

DA FORM 19-24
1 JUN 54

gressive" group within itself. I had no reason to suspect that Adams ever was associated with any secret or clandestine organization. Outside of the other members of the groups in which Adams was involved, I know of no one else who had information relative to his participation. I had no personal knowledge of any mistreatment, abuse, threatening, or placing of additional burdens upon fellow POWs by Adams. I had no personal knowledge of or reason to suspect Adams of having informed on fellow POWs. I had no personal knowledge of any movies, broadcasts, or speeches in which Adams participated, nor of any writings, statement, broadcasts, recordings, or utterances made by Adams relative to germ warfare activities by the United States. I saw Adams in the company of Burchette (fnu) a correspondent for the French Communist newspaper "Le Humu", and Alan Winnington, a correspondent for the "London Daily Worker". However, I had no knowledge of any statements made to these correspondents by Adams. I knew of no statements, writings, broadcasts, recordings, or utterances made by Adams relative to atrocities allegedly engaged in by United States forces. Adams was active in the circulation, sponsoring, and offering for signature to fellow POWs, of various petitions, all of which were derogatory to the United States, although I cannot recall their exact content or to whom the petitions were directed. Adams activity in this matter appeared to be voluntary. I saw articles by Adams in "Towards Truth and Peace", and "Peoples China", Chinese Communist publications circulated within the camp, which were derogatory to the United States, although I do not remember their exact content. I know that Adams received remuneration for his activities in the form of Chinese Communist currency with which he was able to secure such items as cigarettes, wine, and other articles not available to the majority of the POWs. I knew of no staff positions occupied by Adams on any publication nor of any other contribution Adams may have made to other types of publications. I had no personal knowledge of any recordings or broad-

---

AFFIDAVIT BY DEPONENT

I, **Richard Milton Bassett** _____ HAVE HAD READ TO ME (HAVE READ) THIS STATEMENT WHICH BEGINS ON PAGE ONE (1) AND ENDS ON PAGE **3**. I FULLY UNDERSTAND THE CONTENTS OF THE ENTIRE STATEMENT. I HAVE INITIALED ALL CORRECTIONS AND HAVE INITIALED THE BOTTOM OF EACH PAGE WHICH CONTAINS STATEMENT MATTER. THIS STATEMENT WAS MADE BY ME FREELY WITHOUT HOPE OF BENEFIT OR REWARD, WITHOUT THREAT OF PUNISHMENT, AND WITHOUT COERCION, UNLAWFUL INFLUENCE, OR UNLAWFUL INDUCEMENT.

(SIGNATURE OF DEPONENT)

SWORN TO AND SUBSCRIBED BEFORE ME THIS ___ DAY OF **June** 19 **55** AT **Jupiter, Florida**
WITNESSED BY:

Special Agent   Special Agent

(AUTHORITY TO ADMINISTER OATHS)

RIGHTS UNDER UCMJ, ARTICLE 31, AND THE FIFTH AMENDMENT TO THE CONSTITUTION OF THE UNITED STATES

No person subject to this code shall compel any person to incriminate himself or to answer any question the answer to which may tend to incriminate him. No person subject to this code shall interrogate, or request any statement from, an accused or a person suspected of an offense without first informing him of the nature of the accusation and advising him that he does not have to make any statement regarding the offense of which he is accused or suspected and that any statement made by him may be used as evidence against him in a trial by court-martial. No person subject to this code shall compel any person to make a statement or produce evidence before any military tribunal if the statement or evidence is not material to the issue and may tend to degrade him. No statement obtained from any person in violation of this article, or through the use of coercion, unlawful influence, or unlawful inducement shall be received in evidence against him in a trial by court-martial.

The fifth amendment to the Constitution of the United States provides that no person shall be compelled in any criminal case "to be a witness against himself."

DEPONENT'S INITIALS

U. S. GOVERNMENT PRINTING OFFICE : 1954—O—298317

casts made by Adams; however, it was rumored in the camp that Adams had participated in broadcasts. I cannot remember from whom I heard this, having heard it from so many sources, nor do I know the subject or content of these broadcasts. I knew that a group of POWs, including both "progressives" and "reactionaries" left the camp to participate in the filming of a movie but do not recall Adams being among those or any other moving making efforts. Approximately seventy-five (75) percent of the POWs in Camp #5 indulged in the use of marijuana at one time or another, but I cannot recall any occasion upon which Adams used this or any other narcotic. I had no reason to think Adams ever participated in any homosexual or immoral activity or was inclined to such. Adams cooperated with the Chinese Communist camp officials "one hundred per cent" in that he was never known to resist any of their requests or orders. He associated with the camp officials socially, having attended a number of parties given by the Chinese Communists where wine, good food, and females were present. Adams associated with them politically by attending study groups, signing petitions, contributing writings to certain Communist publications mentioned heretofore. I was unable to ascertain Adams motives for his dealings with the Chinese Communists but I venture the opinion that originally it was to receive better treatment. As time advanced and Adams became more involved, I think his participation was due to fear of reprisal from fellow POWs for cooperation with the Chinese or harsh treatment from the Chinese in the event he did not cooperate. Almost without exception the "progressives" who refused to cooperate were treated more harshly than a "reactionary" who refused to obey a like request or order. Adams voluntarily visited the Chinese camp officials in their offices upon their requests. The nature of these visits or what transpired thereat was unknown to me and occurred throughout the entire period of time I knew Adams. This association between Adams and the Chinese Communists was open and all my fellow POWs were aware of it. I know of no military information Adams may have given the Chinese Communists nor do I know of anyone who could furnish any information relative thereto. I know of no effort on Adams' part to avoid repatriation and was rather surprised to find that Adams did not intend to seek repatriation while other "progressives" who had been as seemingly ardent were voluntarily repatriated. I do not think that Adams' actions while in the POW camp were influenced by a depraved state of mind, nor do I think that Adams was mentally subnormal. I can furnish no additional information of acts or events involving Adams.

DOCUMENT 8

On August 16, 1956, the Department of the Army removed Richard Bassett from further "administrative control."

DATE _____ AUG 1 3 ___ 1956

ACSI-SPD-RECAP
SUBJECT: BASSETT, Richard M., US 14206061, C 8050117 (U)

MEMORANDUM FOR RECORD

1. Based upon a review of records developed in the RECAP-K Program it was determined by the ACSI that the subject's file did not contain information of a nature to warrant initiation of action under the provisions of AR 604-10. Subject was removed from administrative control ("flagging action") per Department of the Army letter, subject: "RECAP-K (Part II) Policy Supplement _4_ Annex _J_," dated 31 December 1954.

2. Insofar as this specific RECAP-K action is concerned, future personnel actions may be taken on subject individual without concurrence of or further reference to the Department of the Army.

FOR THE ASSISTANT CHIEF OF STAFF, INTELLIGENCE:

M. A. QUINTO
Colonel, GS
Chief, Security Division

2

ACSI TF 30
4 APRIL 56

DOCUMENT 9

On October 26, 1956, FBI director J. Edgar Hoover declared the evidence "insufficient to establish that [Richard Bassett] violated the treason statute or other applicable federal statutes."

UNITED STATES DEPARTMENT OF JUSTICE
FEDERAL BUREAU OF INVESTIGATION

WASHINGTON 25, D. C.

ply, Please Refer to
No. 100-415057

C 8 0 5 0 1 1 7

Date: October 26, 1956

To: Assistant Chief of Staff, Intelligence
Department of the Army
The Pentagon
Washington 25, D. C.

Attention: Chief, Security Division

From: John Edgar Hoover, Director
Federal Bureau of Investigation

Subject: RICHARD M. BASSETT
TREASON
RECAP K, PART II

Reference is made to my memorandum dated
November 16, 1954.

The Department of Justice has advised that
the material furnished concerning subject's activities
while a prisoner of war in Korea has been reviewed and
it has been determined that the evidence is insufficient
to establish that the subject violated the Treason Statute
or other applicable Federal Statutes.

REGRADED UNCLASSIFIED ON May 18, 1992
BY US DEPT OF JUSTICE
CRIMINAL DIVISION

3

Index